CHANGING VEILS

CHANGING VEILS

Women and Modernisation in North Yemen

CARLA MAKHLOUF

UNIVERSITY OF TEXAS PRESS, AUSTIN

International Standard Book Number 0-292-71049-6
Library of Congress Catalog Card Number 78-72308
Copyright © 1979 Carla Makhlouf

Printed in Great Britain

CONTENTS

CONTENTS

ACKNOWLEDGEMENTS

This book is based mainly on field research in the city of San'a, the capital of North Yemen. As in all research, there are more people to thank than is possible.

I would like to thank Dr Robert Fernea of the Department of Anthropology of the University of Texas at Austin, who gave the initial encouragement for the publication of this book and later contributed many useful comments and suggestions. I am grateful to him, as well as to his wife, Elizabeth Warnock Fernea, for their interest in this project.

I would also like to thank the Center for Behavioral Research at the American University of Beirut and its director Dr E.T. Prothro for a grant covering travel expenses.

I am greatly indebted to the many women in Yemen whose hospitality and kindness made fieldwork an enjoyable are rewarding experience.

Most of all, my gratitude is to my husband. Through his own work on Yemen, he has laid the groundwork for this study and has provided many insights and key ideas as well as constant help and encouragement at all stages of this work.

In the shivers of her clothes are stories
Of yearning and desire and a charming world.
And she sees me from behind the veil,
And I know what is behind the veil.
Is she laughing at me
Or is she smiling to me . . .

(M. Al Sharafī, 1974*)

*M. al Sharafī and A. al Maqálih are contemporary Yemeni poets.
(All translations from Arabic and French are my own.)

To my parents

INTRODUCTION AND BACKGROUND TO THE STUDY

This study tries to understand social change as it is experienced and perceived by women in San'a, the capital city of the Yemen Arab Republic. I have attempted to present a 'multi-dimensional' view of the process of change in its many diverse manifestations, rather than to concentrate on clear indicators of women's 'exploitation' and/or 'emancipation'. As a consequence, the study draws on a variety of sources, mainly, my observations of women's daily routine and ritual activities, of traditional seclusion and veiling patterns, and of modern institutions such as schools, hospitals and the mass media. My other sources of information include statements *by* women interpreting their own lives and their changing society, ideas *about* women and social change as they are expressed in newspaper articles, old legal manuscripts, radio and television programmes, and also some of the provocative work of contemporary Yemeni poets.

As an analysis of females in society, this study makes no claim to be uncovering an ignored subject: for studies of women, almost non-existent in the early seventies, have since then received a great deal of attention. With respect to the Middle East however, and especially the Arabian Peninsula, data and theory are less abundant. Where research has been done, it has concentrated on the most accessible and articulate groups in society, such as college students, educated housewives and women in the labour force. Little is known about females in highly traditional societies except what we can glean from the ethnographies of scholars who, for various reasons, had little or no access to the world of women. Perhaps one virtue of this study is that it focuses on women who have experienced various degrees of seclusion and veiling in a society which, until less than two decades ago, was only known to a few adventurous travellers and audacious merchants — all of them males.

13

For political, economic and religious reasons, Yemen has been historically a most isolated society. Moreover, according to the United Nations,[1] it is one of the six poorest nations of the world. Its Gross National Product was $36 million in 1958 and $811 million in 1973; its per capita income was $126 in 1973; 96 per cent of the Yemeni economy is based on agriculture. Foreign aid totals $432 million (Saint-Hilaire, 1975). The average life expectancy was estimated at 42.3 years in 1965-70 and infant mortality at 40 per cent in 1974. In 1971-2 there were 240 doctors for almost seven million inhabitants and illiteracy was as high as 67.25 per cent (Central Planning Organisation, 1973). Such bare facts have aroused the concern of a legion of aid and development agencies.

However, when we consider cultural achievement, Yemen boasts a tradition of complex architecture and elaborate craftsmanship, of legal sophistication and refined literature, which have flourished in urban centres and are also found in remote tribal areas. All these factors combine to define Yemen as a special case of modernisation and effectively challenge the comfortable notion that traditional culture is a constant in the broad scheme of development.

The central concern of this study is to see the relationship between objective and subjective aspects of social change, to consider not only the objective structural factors as they can be defined by an outside observer but also the subjective reality of change as it is lived and expressed by people in the society. In answering the question of how tradition comes to be questioned, challenged and ultimately transformed, I attempt to keep track of the everyday events as well as crisis points in the lives of the individuals experiencing the 'transition' and dealing with it. Such problems are the concern of much of the work of Peter Berger, and my debt to him will be obvious throughout this book.

The first chapter of this study presents a baseline for an analysis of the dynamics of change in Yemeni society. I define several cultural 'themes' which all relate to a central feature of traditional Yemen: the rigid segregation of the sexes expressed in strict veiling and seclusion practices. I discuss the dominant cultural ideals, the separation of 'male' and 'female' worlds, veiling practices and their meaning, and finally the symbolism of the ritual sphere which perhaps defines a different model of society than that which prevails at the overt level. In juxtaposition to this analysis of tradition, modern forces are discussed in the second chapter with reference to the major changes since the Revolution of 1962, and to the institutions which 'link' women to these macro-level processes. The third chapter examines the process whereby modernising women gradually 'desert' traditional groupings to become members of different types of groups, and learn social relations that are based less on kinship and neighbourhood and more on individualistic factors. As a result, the traditional universe becomes only one among other alternatives for living and rationalising one's life. In the fourth chapter, the aim is to understand how individuals come to adopt ways of life, standards of evaluation and self-perceptions associated with a modern life style. I focus on women who 'migrate' from the traditional to the modern universe, how they feel about their past and present conditions and whether there was a turning point in their lives. Crisis as an area of investigation is used to analyse the emergence of what I refer to as the critical attitude, a crucial element in the process of modernisation. I also examine prevalent ideas about women in the mass media and literature as they express and project changing attitudes and patterns of behaviour.

Fieldwork for the study was completed during July-August 1974 and March-June 1976. Significantly enough, the first two months were those following the bloodless coup by Colonel al Hamdi and his Corrective Movement, *Al Ḥaraka al Taṣḥīhiya*. The new regime vehemently expressed its concern for development in all spheres of life and declared its encouragement of women's participation in the process of modernisation. This political transformation lends special value to a study which aims at understanding social changes in relation to critical experiences. After completing the initial stage of the research in 1974, I was afforded the opportunity to return to San'a in March 1976, this time at the height of the Lebanese internal war. The realities of crisis in the Middle East have thus constituted a constant and dramatic backdrop to the study — for better and for worse.

The opportunity to restudy the problem of change helped me to verify a number of hypotheses formulated earlier concerning the significance of veiling, changing seclusion patterns, the importance of crisis points, such as divorce, in the women's modernising experience, the consequences of increased alternatives for life-planning and the disruption of the traditional universe. I was also able to take advantage of earlier contacts and to follow the 'life-careers' of some of my informants over a period of eighteen months. Moreover, having access to many homes and being party to the inside gossip and rumours of female networks, I felt less of an outsider to the culture and more confident about my data and analysis.

The initial study of 1974[2] focused on a sample of forty women interviewed more or less systematically, depending on the context and the circumstances. The interviewing technique was not formal or structured. Rather, I made every effort to stimulate conversation on topics that were deemed relevant both to the women and to the research, without making the situation unnatural or boring to any of us. Group interviews were conducted where the situation presented itself. In general, interviews were 'minimally structured'[3] and the approach was to stay within the bounds of ordinary conversation while encouraging each woman to express her views about various fields of social life and to give her evaluation of social patterns.

Table 1 gives some information about my initial sample. Of the 40 women, 15 were interviewed three times or more. Where they appear in the text, figures refer to this sample; data collected later are added for comparison.

Unavoidable aspects of any fieldwork, circumstances of association as well as chance factors undoubtedly influenced the nature of my sample. Most of my informants belong to the upper and middle social strata of San'a. As a result, the image of women's life presented here is an urban one. I did travel around the country and spent time with both rural and tribal women.[4] I am aware of the great differences between their lives and those of urban women. Tribal and rural women are not subjected to such strict seclusion patterns as

Introduction

Table 1: Background Data on Women Interviewed

---

a. *Age:*

Range	Number
11-15	5
16-20	15
21-25	12
26-30	3
31-40	3
41+	2
	40

b. *Marital status:*

Single	15
Married	16 (4 as second wives)
Divorced	6
Widowed	3
	40

c. *Education:*

Level	Number	Per cent
None	10	25
Literate	5	12.5
Primary	8	20
Secondary	17	42.5
	40	100

d. *Occupation:*

	Number	Per cent
Housewife	20	50
Student	9	22.5
Employed	11	27.5
	40	100

e. *Marital status of employed women:*

Widowed	1
Never married*	1
Unmarried	3
Married	3
Divorced	3
	11

---

* By 'never married' I mean unmarried and past marrying age.

the women in San'a, since kinship provides the main if not the only context of social interaction. In spite of this, or more correctly, because of this, rural and tribal women have far fewer opportunities for interaction and hence manipulation of social encounters. Moreover, the Yemeni countryside is to a large extent without running water, electricity and a road network; life conditions burden the women doubly with household chores and work in the fields. This study makes no claim to generalise about Yemeni women as a whole, nor even San'ani women.

One advantage of an urban middle-class and upper-class sample, however, is that such women have been most exposed to change and their problems in confronting traditional patterns highlight the main areas of conflict between tradition and modernity in Yemen. Also, as an elite group, they are likely to be emulated by others, to act as brokers of ideas and patterns of behaviour, and to constitute some kind of avant-garde which can influence the process of change in their society.

Notes

1. All figures, except where otherwise indicated, are from the United Nations *Statistical Yearbooks*.

2. Since most of the systematic work of sampling and interviewing was completed in the first period of the fieldwork, I have chosen not to alter the data and figures which I had collected then, but to add comparable data from the second part of the fieldwork.

3. This may seem too casual an approach. But the more structured technique of interviewing was tried and proved to be less than successful. The result was laconic and awkward answers on the part of the informant, and on the researcher's part created a feeling of artificiality and even a sense of betrayal of friendly patterns established earlier.

4. Comparative data are based on short stays with selected key informants in villages of the area bordering South Yemen, towns and villages of the highland plains south of San'a and tribal areas and towns of the eastern desert plains around the ancient city of Ma'reb.

1 THE TRADITIONAL SETTING

'For we are women,
And we are finished
Even before life begins'.

(M. al Sharafī, 1970).

The distinction implied in this chapter between tradition and modernity is not made on the basis of a dividing point in time, even though the Revolution of 1962 provides a special date; nor is it assumed that tradition is the sum of internal, and modernity that of external, elements, even though this is to some extent true. In other words, tradition and modernity are not seen as independent systems of mechanically related variables, but as two aspects of one historical process.

I have selected a few aspects of traditional culture for discussion. These do not follow the usual division of social life into sectors such as kinship, economics, politics and religion. They have been selected not only because they were felt to be crucial for understanding traditional culture from the point of view of the female, but also because they all stimulate reflection of one important problem, that of the relation between the 'male aspect' and the 'female aspect' of the culture. In other words, social reality is seen here as the product of a dialectic between two opposed tendencies within the culture, the one 'male', the other one 'female'.

Up to a certain time, most of the literature about sex roles in Arab society either explicitly discussed or else implied the notion of the dominant status of the male and the subordinate status of the female (Antoun, 1968 and 1972; Baer, 1964; Fuller, 1961; Lutfiyya, 1966; Patai, 1973; Tillion, 1966); whereas more recent studies and accounts indicate that it is possible for the woman to have some decision-making power (Fernea, 1969 and 1976; Maher, 1974; Nelson, 1974; Altorki, 1973). The point here is that each of the two theoretical trends touches on one level of the culture: the former, that of overt ideology and action, the latter, that of inner structure. It is significant that earlier studies were more often conducted by researchers who, because of their particular role and status, had limited access to the women's world, and more recent ones by fieldworkers who succeeded in gaining an entree to the more secluded domains of social life. It is the aim here to combine these two perspectives and attempt to reveal some aspects of the interaction between the overt and covert levels of the culture.

I. The Politico-Religious Ideology in Yemeni Culture

The political ideology of Yemen emerges from the interaction of historical, religious and political factors. Historically, the North of the country was tribally organised and even today tribal divisions, alliances and confederations remain important. Moreover, the country has been dominated by the followers of the Zaidi sect which emerged in Iraq at the end of the Umayyad period and became dominant in Yemen by the eleventh century. According to Zaidi doctrine, as expounded in *Kitāb al Azhār*, the main treatise, legitimacy of rule is based upon fourteen requirements, among which are: being a male, a descendant of Ali, learned in religious matters and capable of leading his followers in holy battle. Both Zaidism and tribalism stress certain values which seem to celebrate the activities and virtues of men in groups and to restrict achievement in the political sphere to the males.[1] Moreover, in the religious courts of Yemen, as in tribal law, the blood money (*diya*) paid for a woman is evaluated at half the amount paid for a man, and the testimony of a man is worth that of two women.

The exclusion of the female at the legal level may in fact be the cultural expression of her seclusion at the social level, her restriction to the domestic sphere and her lack of access to public decision-making. Before the Revolution of 1962, education for the female was restricted to reading the Korān and did not include writing, except for a few upper-class women. One informant stated that traditional San'anis did not want girls to know how to write, because they might start writing letters to people. Still today in Yemen, schoolgirls represent only 9 per cent of the total number of pupils and 1.6 per cent of the girls in the age group concerned. The illiteracy rate for the total population of Yemen is estimated at 90 per cent (United Nations, 1973). Moreover, until very recently women were not allowed to work outside the house and were thus limited to familial roles defined by the rights and duties of the kinship system. The public image of the woman was mostly a function of her stage in the life-cycle and a reflection of the status of her husband. Outside these two factors, there were no major bases for status differentiation. In spite of the minor differences, women could be lumped into one category, *al ḥarīm* (the women). This seems to concur with Simmel's suggestion that 'the most general of her qualities, the fact that she was a woman and as such served the functions proper to her sex caused her to be classified with all other women under one general concept' (1955, p. 180). All women led similar lives, characterised by a domestic orientation and a strict segregation of male and female spheres of action.

II. Women's Separate Sphere

In a society marked by strict seclusion and rigidly defined sex roles, one would expect to find that the behaviour of women is extremely constrained. In fact, one of the most striking features of female society in Yemen is the atmosphere of relaxation which seems to prevail during both work and leisure time.

I visited some San'ani houses at different times of the day to observe the unfolding of the daily routine. In the morning, the men are always absent from home; they spend time at the office, the shop, the market or the mosque. During that time, the house is completely a female domain. The women do their cooking, cleaning, laundry. They receive brief visits from friends who drop by to inquire about something, extend an invitation to an afternoon visit, or simply to exchange news and chat a little.

Around the time of the noon prayer, men return home. In households of one nuclear family, all eat the midday meal together; if there are guests, or if the houshold includes a large number of relatives, the men eat first, and later the women and children. The meal typically includes a dish of bread soaked in yoghurt, a dish of pastry covered with honey, a dish of *ḥelba* (a sort of sorghum pounded with spices and meat juice), some cooked meat and some fruit. There is little variation from this standard menu.

Usually, a normal small family lunch takes only a short time, and children are allowed to eat as much — or as little — as they wish. After the meal is over, the man goes out again, sometimes to work, most often to a gathering of friends for music and *qāt*-chewing.[2]

Women's lunches, like the rest of their activities, are casual. A tablecloth is laid on the floor, and pots, baskets, dishes, loaves of bread and salad leaves are arranged on it in a most pleasant fashion. All guests sit on the floor around the tablecloth — there seems to be no 'placing' of guests. Everybody reaches for the dishes as they are brought in, pieces of bread and silverware are informally passed around. Each eats at his own pace, which is usually fast, and people get up as soon as they have had enough to eat, regardless of those still eating. After clearing up, the women sit together in another room; incense is passed around to perfume the hair and colognes are generously poured on the heads of guests. Then coffee, *qishr*[3] and tea are offered.

The afternoon prayer defines the beginning of an important female ritual. Around three o'clock, in the streets of San'a, one may begin to see groups of girls and women veiled in black going to a *tafrita* (afternoon visit), some carrying their *qāt* wrapped in big pieces of bright plastic.[4] At the same time, men also are going to friends' houses to chew *qāt*. It is usually arranged in advance that the men of the household receive their guests when the women are invited out, and, conversely, the women manage to invite their friends on days when the men are out. Afternoon visits constitute the principal leisure activity in Yemeni society. Many of the women's *tafriṭa* are held to mark important events like births or marriages, but often they are not directly related to such 'rites of passage' and sociability is their apparent motive.[5]

Usually, a very large number of women are gathered at a *tafriṭa*, and I have rarely been to one where the reception room was less than overcrowded. Sometimes there are so many guests that those already sitting on the carpets have to squeeze together to make room for newcomers. Guests arrive all veiled in black, remove their cloaks and shoes at the door, and appear in the *majlis* (sitting room) dressed in various colours of rich brocades and velvets or the cheaper cloths and synthetics which mark the lower status groups. The women wear their best clothes and display their jewelry, especially if the *tafriṭa* is a more ritual one, or one taking place at a richer woman's. All wear bright muslin scarves on their heads, and married women wear a brocade band around the forehead. Upon entering a women's *majlis*, one is taken by the glimmer of all the colours and brocades, by the chatter and music, the pungent smell of tobacco, the heady scent of incense, the sweet fragrance of perfume, and the hot damp atmosphere of the room.

The space in the middle of the *majlis* is taken up by several tall brass *madā'* (waterpipe or hookah) whose long hoses sinuate across the room and are passed among the guests. Tea and *qishr*, spicy, hot and sweet, are passed around as well as nuts, raisins, candy, and, a surprising intruder among all these traditional items rich in feminine and masculine connotations, *ṭuffāsh* (popcorn). Women enjoy smoking the *madā'* and about one third chew *qāt* which, they say, cools the body and relaxes it after the fatigues of the day. There may be some riddle-guessing, story-telling and joking at a *tafriṭa*. Always there is music. If a professional singer is present she will take her tambourine and sing, but most often now she has been replaced by the cassette-player which brings into San'ani houses the songs of popular Egyptian, Syrian and Lebanese musicians as well as the famous local and Adeni lute players and singers. Then some women get up, clear some space in the middle of the room by removing discarded *qāt* leaves and trays of coffee-cups, and dancing begins. San'ani dances, distinct from other tribal or local dances, consist in subtle movements of the feet, hips and arms, following a melody which at first sounds monotonous, but which, as one learns to follow the evasive rythm and the complex, contrapuntal structure, becomes enchanting.

The evening prayer marks the end of the *tafriṭa* and the time when both men and women go back to their homes. Since there is no evening dinner, as the intake of *qāt* considerably reduces the appetite, the return from visiting seems to end the daily cycle of activities.

There is little variety in the regular daily routine. Fridays and feast days hardly differ from other days, except perhaps in the amount of visiting. Generally, the women's lives follow a repetitive pattern limited to the house, and marked by the absence of privacy. While the men are busy in the market, the office and the mosque, involved in those economic, political and religious activities that are defined as central in the culture, the domestic orientation of women seems irrelevant to the progression of activities 'outside' in the society. As if, by so clearly defining the feminine space, culture were setting women apart into timelessness . . .

The all-female groupings that exist as a result of seclusion constitute the universe within which girls and women of all ages spend the greatest part of their lives. From the time of childhood, girls to a greater extent than boys are likely to participate in an inter-generational world with their mothers, aunts and grandmothers. Very early they begin to help with household chores and attend to their younger siblings. Always when I was visiting my San'ani informants in the morning, there would be a younger sister or an eldest daughter working in the kitchen, grinding the greens and spices for the daily dish of *ḥelba*, cutting vegetables, going on little errands or supervising the play of younger children. Young boys, on the other hand, are usually left to play all day with their friends in the streets or occasionally accompany their fathers to the market or the mosque.[6] Little girls are encouraged very early to learn the role of women; they often accompany their mothers on afternoon visits, and some of them are even eager to start wearing the black cloak and veil before the prescribed age of ten. The socialisation of little girls takes place within the context of groupings character-ised by particularistic, diffuse, affective relationships and seems to favour continuity rather than fragmentation in the development of personality.[7] This helps moderate the impact of transitions in the life cycle and dampens the possibilities of inter-generational conflict, but at the same time it rein-forces traditional ideas and practices.

The traditional woman's world, then, offers little chance for achievement. The only roles open to women are those defined by their position in the life cycle, and the activities which delimit these roles have no special cultural value attached to them. In the standard Zaidi legal treatise *Kitāb al Azhār*, written in the fifteenth century AD and the main reference on all matters relating to *sharī'a* (Islamic law), it is stated that the only duty of women is to allow sexual intercourse (*tamkīn al waṭ'*). This was later amended by Imam Ahmed (1948-62) who added that women should not stay idle and that it was also their duty to work in the house (*Ikhtiyārāt al Imām Ahmed*, n.d.).[8]

The cultural ideology, however, does not always provide a complete picture of social reality. In this case, where there exists a large amount of sex segregation, women are given a separate sphere over which men have little control and which may constitute a source of support and even of power.[9]

This separate sphere also provides a source of information and gossip in a society which encourages secrecy about the home and about women (both are sometimes referred to by the same term, *al ḥaram*). One may even argue that daily visits represent for women a public domain of activity, if we mean by public that sphere of life which is situated at the inter-familial level. Women's access to this public sphere counterbalances the domestic orientation by which they are otherwise defined. It is possible, as will become clear later, for women to manipulate this sphere in order to influence decision-making and thus gain some informal political importance in society. In other words, the restriction of the female to the domestic sphere, which characterises Yemeni patrilineal society, is only partial.

Moreover, a cultural ideology which presents women's part in society as insignificant does not necessarily result in self-devaluation for the women.[10] Rather, the subjective reality of women's lives may contradict this view. In fact, for the outsider expecting constrained and repressed female types as a result of seclusion, it is a most agreeable surprise to find that San'ani women do not seem nearly as tense or inhibited as women in some other cultures. Almost always the atmosphere at women's gatherings is pleasant and relaxing. Housework is accepted as part of being a woman. One informant when asked whether she liked it replied simply:

'If I didn't like it they [meaning her husband and children] wouldn't eat.' It should also be pointed out that San'ani women's housework constitutes less of a burden than that of many Western housewives, even though there are no machines to help with the work. Given the simplicity of the furniture, which consists of cushions, carpet and brasses, a San'ani house is rather easy to care for. Also, since chewing *qāt* in the afternoon diminishes the appetite, Yemenis do not usually take an evening meal. Thus women's work ends with lunch and they have every afternoon free for going to a visit: the amount of time spent on housework seems less in urban Yemen than in many other cultures.[11] Looking after children is reduced to a minimum and child-rearing patterns are very permissive; children are not given a great deal of surveillance and are left to play with neighbours' children in the street. A further point is that household chores are shared by the girls and women of the house without a strict division of tasks, which allows for a lot of flexibility. Tasks are performed at a very relaxed pace, the boundary between work and leisure is not very rigid. Yet although the woman's schedule allows for moments of relaxation, it is both repetitive and uneventful.

The afternoon visit offers both a daily diversion from the routine of the household cycle and a ritual focus which confers meaning on the life of women. It is not merely one of the activities of the day, it is in many cases a right that women can claim. Men may complain that 'all women do is go to *tafriṭa*', but they do not seem to be able to change the pattern. *Tafriṭa* is an integral part of the women's lives. Its colourful, stimulating character contrasts with the dullness of the morning and provides entertainment, pleasant sensations and a feeling of euphoria due to the combination of heat, smoke, *qāt* and music. To a certain extent, behaviour at the *tafriṭa* is governed by etiquette, but is is never too formalised: there is always some joking, laughing and light chatting.

The social conditions of *tafriṭa* are such that they seem to stress nearness and community rather than discordance. Since it is common for over fifty women to be sitting on the floor in a room of three by six metres, perspiring and smoking together, one obvious result is that status differences will appear to be less relevant. In other words, the absence of physical distance seems to prevent the building of social distance and contributes to what Simmel refers to as the 'democratic nature of sociability' which is 'the game in which one "does as if" all were equal' (1950, p. 49). What this crowdedness emphasises is, if not the equality, at least the sense of community of the participants. And actually, status differences are not great, because they are only marked by subtle variations in types of cloth, brocades, velvets or jewelry. In other words *tafriṭa* provides a daily drama which pretends to ignore dissonance and conflict, and hence may serve to reinforce existing social conditions.

The dramatic nature of *tafriṭa* is expressed in another characteristic, also related to the physical and spatial structure of the ritual. Given the large number present, women may at any moment leave the main room for another to cool off and chat with other women. The atmosphere in the latter room is always more informal, and provides some relief from both material and social restraints. To use Goffman's terms, it constitutes a backstage in relation to the dramatic nature of the main *majlis* as a frontstage. In the traditional *tafriṭa*, when they are not making jokes, telling stories or dancing, women are engaged in conversation about children, husbands, close and distant relatives, recent marriages, births or divorces, which are topics of common interest and tend to reinforce female identity and community. But conversation is not only verbal exchange; it has also a silent language. Equally important is the implicit part of the conversation, the fact that it takes for granted, or perhaps pretends, that participants belong to the same social world. Thus, it may provide a means of expressing, without verbalising, potential unity, and may reaffirm the reality of the culture.[12]

The functions of *tafriṭa*, both manifest (as entertainment) and latent (as a means of communication and as a bonding ritual) contribute to giving it a central place in traditional life. It is the point around which the other activities of traditional women revolve, the most enjoyable and perhaps the most meaningful. It also provides participants with satisfaction — and frustrations — that are independent of men's attitudes and evaluations. Women dress up for the visits, they show off their jewelry and dance, but not to seduce the men, who can never be present. *Tafriṭa* is the symbol of a female world possessing a certain degree of autonomy from the world of males, and the absence of the veil during visits is a symbolic reminder of this autonomy. This separate world may be a 'part society', but its members do not seem to view it as incomplete just because they are excluded from the male world.[13]

One may go even further, and attempt to turn upside down the commonsense 'truth' which contends that the women are excluded from the male world. One can venture that in fact the men are excluded from the female world, as much, if not more, than females are excluded from the world of the men. A number of observations would support this view. First, there is a marked difference in speech patterns of men and women which makes it difficult for a man to understand when women speak among themselves. Men's speech is closer to classical Arabic and easier to understand for women and for a non-Yemeni, whereas women speak with a guttural but high-pitched voice and at a higher speed.[14] A number of men have actually told me that they could not understand women's language.[15] I myself had greater trouble at first getting used to the women's particular dialect, whereas I could understand men's conversation almost without trouble. It is thus not too far-fetched to suggest that men are somewhat more excluded from an understanding of the world of the opposite sex.

Also, men's infringement of the female separate sphere is prevented by an 'early warning system'. Usually, one house is reserved for the men's afternoon visit, and another for the women's. However, I have seen it happen that a man enters his house while there is a female gathering there. In this case, he is required to say 'Allah! Allah!' loudly a number of times while climbing the stairs of his house,[16] so that the women, hearing him, are able to change their comportment and cover their faces before he sees them. This exclusion ritual is in contrast to the simpler and more common entry of a veiled female into an all-male social group — for instance, to serve meals to the males of the household and their guests. Through serving meals, a female can learn a lot about males' gatherings. Some informants told me about these gatherings, not just who was present but also what the conversation was about. Conversely, a man can never see a female gathering under normal conditions since his very presence completely changes the definition of the situation.

One exception worth mentioning is a Yemeni singer and comedian whom I interviewed. He is very popular in both male and female social circles for his imitations, parodies and songs. This man was proud to tell how he was the only male to have seen the women's *tafriṭa* under normal conditions. This happened when he was hired for entertaining a large group of females. The interesting thing is that he had to disguise himself as a female, and that, even though all the women knew who he was, they did not put on their veils, and the visit went on as if no male were present. This event is most suited for a Goffmanesque analysis since it shows the interaction between the definition of the situation and the actors' performance. But it also indicates the persistence of some aspects of the caste-like social structure of traditional Yemeni culture where the role of singer (*dawshān*), along with others such as barber-circumciser (*muzayyin*), and female beautician-hairdresser (*shāri'a*), belongs to an inferior social category which is sometimes exempt from cultural rules of segregation. The fact that the rules governing veiling practices could be relaxed in the presence of the singer indicates that in spite of his identification with modern success (he had worked for Kuwait Television for a couple of years and the cassettes he records are 'bestsellers' in San'a), he was still classified into the traditional category of *dawshān*. The point is that no man belonging to the same social category as the women, would have been allowed to break the norm as the singer did.[17] In other words, a violation of the rule preventing men from entering the world of women, and protecting the sacredness of the *ḥaram* or *ḥarīm* (interchangeable here) is associated with loss of status, or with ambivalent status, for the trespasser. Whereas for a woman who enters an all-male group the veil provides a convenient means of being present without her presence being acknowledged, and seeing without being seen.

However, the frequently expressed notion that the veil

depersonalises the person wearing it is only a partial aspect of reality.[18] Of course, one probable consequence of the veil is that the veiled person is experienced as a 'non-person', to use Goffman's term, by those not acquainted with the culture. But it is not a necessary consequence that the veiled persons themselves feel depersonalised or are treated by men as non-persons.[19] One should take into consideration not only the objective reality of veiling patterns, but also their subjective reality, not only what veiling consists in, but also how it is experienced by the women themselves: this is the problem we shall consider now.

III. The Veil: Social Reality and Symbolism

What is generally referred to as the veil consists in fact of several parts, each having a special name and usage. Of the two types of headcovers worn indoors, only one, the *lithma*, is a veil in the real sense. The other is not used to conceal the face, but only the hair, and apparently more for purposes of fashion and elegance than veiling. It is a long square or rectangular scarf of brightly-coloured, sometimes printed muslin, worn over the head and shoulders, with a band of brocade tied around the forehead. This type of headscarf is worn by married women on afternoon visits. The actual 'indoor veil', the *lithma*, is worn by unmarried girls at all times and by married women in daily routines of house-work or for informal morning visits. The *lithma* is a piece of brightly-coloured thin material or muslin draped around the head in such a way as to cover the hair and the forehead, while the lower part of it can be pulled down to uncover or pulled up to cover the whole face except the eyes, according to changes in the definition of the situation. When there are no men around, the *lithma* is down but a woman must cover her face in the presence of a man who is not her husband and is not covered by the incest taboo.[20] The *lithma* is used when a man unexpectedly enters the room where women are gathered.

The 'outdoor veil' is of two types. The first is the *sitāra*, a large piece of cotton material printed in red, blue and green, and covering the head and the body. To this is added a piece of black batik ornamented with large red and white

circles covering the face and transparent enough to let the
woman see through. The other type of outdoor veil, the
sharshaf, consists of three parts: a long pleated skirt worn
over the dress and a waist-length cape covering the head and
shoulders, both made of black silk-like material, and a piece
of thin black muslin to cover the face, the *khunna*. Women
of the lower social categories tend to wear the *sitāra* whereas
those of higher rank wear the black *sharshaf*; some women of
the middle social categories alternate between the two,
wearing the *sitāra* for casual occasions such as morning
errands and visits to immediate neighbours, and wearing
the *sharshaf* for afternoon visits. All women and all girls
above ten have to wear either the *sitāra* or the *sharshaf* when
they go out of the house. The only unveiled women in the
streets are the non-Yemeni, some Yemeni women born in
East Africa, and the women who belong to the *akhdām*, the
lowest category in the Yemen.[21] The fact that the
akhdām do not wear the veil might be related to the general
notion of the veil as a status symbol and the account of its
emergence as a distinctive sign worn by the women of the
Prophet's family to ensure that they be recognised in public
and left unbothered.[22]

There is another kind of headcover worn by women which
is also related to status, but in a different manner. The
qirqāsh or *qarqūsh* is a little hood made of brocade which
was worn until recently. Nowadays it has been abandoned,
and women consider it old-fashioned, even laughable. Only
little girls below the age of ten can be seen wearing it when
playing in the street. But there is an interesting exception to
this practice. At several *tafriṭa*, I repeatedly met one old maid
who still wears the *qarqūsh*. One informant told me that she
had no family to support her and lived off the charity of
other women. The latter's attitude towards her is a mixture
of benevolence and mockery, of kindness and ridicule. One
may suggest here, using Douglas's term (1966), that this old
maid is an 'anomaly' in a society where all the girls marry.
She would therefore tend to arouse a kind of 'anxiety', all
the more so since having no kin relatives in a society where
kinship is the basis of social relationships, she has no clear
role to play. Hence, the slight — probably unconscious —

embarrassment, and its expression or suppression by laughter. Hence also, the charitable attitude which at one level is a manifestation of the humaneness of the community towards its less fortunate members, and at another level serves to perpetuate the character of this woman as a symbol of the boundary between the normal and the anomalous. It is not surprising then that the old maid would wear the old-fashioned *qirqāsh* which signals her as standing outside, in a way behind, the cultural practices of the majority.

Kinds of headcover and patterns of veiling, then, function as indicators of the social condition of individuals in a society where there exists a high degree of congruence between the different roles of one individual, and also between social status and its subtle manifestations in clothing. And the veil, though it is obviously a restriction on communication, may be seen in another perspective as constituting in itself a communicative device for making symbolic statements.

The veil does not prevent women from recognising friends and relatives in the street or from chatting together when they meet. Women can identify one another through various signs such as differences in stature and particular mannerisms. By moving around with women, I began gradually to learn how to recognise people without seeing their faces. Moreover, for someone acquainted with the culture, the veil itself can express subtle differences, such as those between the various social categories, especially with respect to wearing the *sharshaf* or the *sitāra*. There are other outward indicators of status, such as the very material used for the veil. Even though the *sharshaf* is always black, the material can be of good or bad quality and it can be plain or embroidered with black flowers. Also, the black skirt can be made to appear more or less fashionable: one young woman had it cut slightly differently (a little tighter and longer) so that it looked, as she said, like a fashionable 'maxi' skirt.

Thus, though veiling certainly constitutes an obstacle to the free expression of women as persons, and a device which, at least apparently, reduces all women to anonymous figures, it is not simply that. Beyond casual appearances, there are aspects of veiling which enhance rather than obstruct the expression of self and femininity. Concealing the body is primarily done for purposes of modesty but it can also be provocative: 'The social distance imposed by the covering enhances what is already seen as feminine in the culture: sexuality, a special sense of vulnerability and an inability to move freely in public' (Papanek, 1973, p. 296). Concealing can be provocative because it evokes its opposite, revealing. In the daily newspaper *Al Thawra* one opponent of the veil used precisely this argument: he wrote that the *sharshaf* had ceased to be a modest garment and that it 'showed' the charms of the women by so strongly evoking them. The husband of one of my informants told me that what had first attracted him to her was a short glimpse he had of her face when she once happened to lift her veil. There are statements which echo this one in popular Arabic songs or poems, even all the way back to the traditional genre of *ghazal* (love poetry) in classical Arabic poetry. What is seen after being concealed is all the more attractive, for the veil clothes women in an aura of mystery and contributes to the imagery of the ideal woman.

By making all women look alike, the veil provides a certain freedom of movement: a veiled woman could go with men and have affairs without being caught. As one man pointed out, people may think she is walking with a man covered by the incest taboo, whereas if her face were not concealed, her relatives would know who she is, and that she should not be walking in the street with this man. One informant who was quite knowledgeable about illicit relations in San'a by virtue of the fact that she dealt both personally and officially with the problems of urban women told me that many upper-class married women had secret affairs which it was difficult for the husband to discover because the veil provides a means of going places 'incognito'. In other words, even though a woman who breaches the moral code may be recognised by friends or relatives, her veil can be used as a disguise, to provide an element of doubt against accusations.

Thus, the veil is not just an obstacle, a static reality, it is not merely a given, it can also be manipulated. We have mentioned how women use the *lithma* to cover their faces when a man unexpectedly comes into the house. What is interesting is that the women do not take the whole situation too seriously and that the supposedly dramatic character of the intrusion is attenuated by its being considered comical. After hearing the signal of the man's entry, all women, laughing, pull up their *lithma*. Some of them — accidentally or purposely — are incapable of concealing their faces quickly enough. It may be that they had taken off the *lithma* altogether and cannot drape it back quickly enough. Then, to the amusement of all the women present, they hurriedly try to drape it, or look for another piece of material, or hide their face behind their neighbour. Goffman's discussion of team-mates versus audience is appropriate here:

> When team-mates are warned that the audience is approaching, the team-mates may hold off their performance, purposely, until the very last minute, until the audience almost catches a glimpse of backstage activity. Similarly, the team may race into backstage relaxation the moment the audience has departed. By means of this rapid switch into or out of their act, the team in a sense can contaminate and profanize the audience by backstage conduct . . . or make extremely clear the difference between team and audience, and do all of these things without quite being caught out by the audience. (Goffman, 1971, p. 172)

Goffman's observations concur with my idea that seclusion and veiling function as much to exclude men as to seclude women. Goffman's remark that the team thus 'rebels against the obligation of maintaining a show before the audience' (loc. cit.) can also explain another pattern of behaviour related to veiling. All girls above the age of ten have to wear either the *sitāra* or the *sharshaf* whenever they leave the house. I have observed that, should a girl wish to walk the short distance between her house and that of a friend or relative, she may borrow a piece of material to cover her head and shoulders. Then giggling all the way, she will run the short distance separating the two entrance doors. This behaviour is very similar to that of the girl who fails to cover her face in time in that both have the same quality of playfulness in evading the rule.

There are other ways to evade the strict norms of veiling,

and, through observing girls in general and my own informants in particular, I became aware of the subtle ways in which girls can breach the rules without incurring sanctions. Thus, it is generally accepted that a woman may lift her *khunna* for a very short instant in case she needs to look at something or someone at a distance or when she is announcing herself at a door; some girls, taking advantage of this, will purposely lift the *khunna* earlier and draw it down later than necessary, so that their faces are uncovered for a slightly longer time than usual — especially if there are men around. Similary, I once watched one of my informants go down the inside stairs of a house without covering her face when she knew that there were men on the lower levels of the house and even on the stairs — then she covered her face in feigned surprise. Another time, some of my friends took me to watch the 'male side' of a wedding that was being celebrated that evening.[23] The groom was ritually leaving his father's house to go to the bride's and bring her, and all the men were gathered in the street, singing the traditional wedding songs. One of my friends lifted her veil to look at the men and started commenting upon their physical appearance, comparing one to an Indian movie actor, another to her uncle, and giggling all the time. Some of the men noticed her and began looking up to where we were standing. Other women knew this girl as 'one of those who lift their veil and let men see their face', and they spoke of her with amusement and not severe disapproval.

Another of my informants was also a 'veil manipulator', but in a different way. She had a maternal cousin (*ibn khāla*) whom she 'considered as a brother'. He lived with her family for a while and during that time she did not veil in his presence; she used to wash and cook for him and tried to please him 'as she would a brother'. But after she heard that he wanted to marry her, she started wearing the veil and doing things he disliked. In this instance she used the veil to establish social distance, discourage a relationship which she did not desire, and declare her freedom of choice. Thus, the veil, in principle a restriction on freedom, can be used to affirm independence by making statements about social distance.[24]

It is interesting that none of my informants when questioned about the veil mentioned the frequently expressed idea that the veil is a cause or a manifestation of the female's inferior status. The women did not seem to think in these terms, even when directly questioned about the idea. Those who disapproved of veiling did not relate their position to the idea of the veil as a symbol of inferiority. They objected to the veil because they considered it cumbersome, meaningless, and an obstacle to sincere interaction between the sexes. On the other hand, some women were in favour of the veil. One of them wrote an article in the daily paper arguing that the veil did not hinder the education of the female or the development of the country, pointing out that veiled girls do go to school, that veiled women do work in the textile factory or in offices, and concluded: 'The technical development of those who reached the moon was certainly not due to their women being unveiled'. She thought that the free-mixing of the sexes was not necessary for the education of the female. Implied in her opinions is the traditional notion that the female's separate sphere is a somewhat autonomous and self-sufficient world.

Another woman had a different approach to the problem. She had studied at the university in Cairo and, back in Yemen, was for a while the president of the Yemeni Woman's Association. Yet in spite of her position she wore both the *sharshaf* and the *lithma*. When I asked her why she did so, she answered that the veil was not a cause of women's inferior status. She considered the issue of the veil as secondary when compared to those of early marriage, high fertility, illiteracy and lack of any activity outside housework and *tafriṭa*. For the time being, it was not deemed urgent, according to her, to deal with the veil: other things had to change first. She argued that the veil still provided some protection in a traditional society and that the costs of taking it off would be too high. Most of my other informants said that the veil did not bother them but that it was a protection against the looks of men; they thought that if they were unveiled, men would stare at them and think bad things, and their reputations would suffer. One of them said, for instance: 'Men generalise about women and if one unveiled woman [*mutabarrija* or *fātsha*] is dirty and behaves improperly, they would think that all unveiled women are the same. So when all women unveil, we shall unveil too, but this will take time.'

In fact, the social pressures on those who want to reject the veil are enormous. One woman told me that she had decided not to wear the veil any more, but the tension was such that she could only last one year, after which she found it easier to conform. Another woman, the head of the San'a nursing school, explained that men themselves are undecided about the veil: some may in theory agree that it should not exist, but when it comes to women of their own family, they enforce the traditional norm. The reaction of women is no less equivocal: when asked whether some girls did in fact take off their veils, some of my informants replied that this was impossible, or if it really happened, then the girls must be 'mad' (*majnūna*), or 'stupid' (*mā fī 'aql*). Then, only a few minutes later, the same women were joking about girls who lift their veil in the street.

From all of this, I would argue that people's attitudes towards the veil can only be ambivalent, because the veil itself is an ambivalent part of the everyday drama of social relations and a component of all encounters. To reject the veil altogether would be a complete denial of a 'performance' which is essential to social life. Whoever refuses to veil places herself outside of the normative order, just like 'idiots' and 'madmen'. On the other hand, girls who playfully lift their veils in the street are not as severely condemned. Playing with the veil does not contest the validity of the practice itself, since it is an abrupt occurrence after which the performance is resumed. What is more, playful evasion of rules lends to the routine performance the thrill of a minor breach and the excitement of a game, thus rendering it even more dramatic.

While the veil is a central element in the culture, San'anis in general — both male and female — are aware of the contingency of the practice. The veil is not worn in most villages of the countryside, nor by *'akhdām* women, nor Yemeni women from East Africa nor foreign women. In fact, unlike other countries such as Saudi Arabia, no foreign woman is expected to veil. One time I mentioned to my friends that I was thinking of going out in the street wearing a *lithma*; they started to laugh and then seriously said: 'No, you are a foreigner, you should not do that, people would laugh at you.' Moreover, in Yemeni families living abroad, the women never veil though they do upon returning to Yemen. Thus there is a diffuse awareness that veiling is contingent upon other factors. Along with modernisation there emerges a more explicit attitude of relativism towards traditional norms and scepticism towards the veiling performance in particular.

The veil, it has been noted, is important in societies where concern for descent and group solidarity reinforces male honour as a central value and where 'women's proper behaviour as sheltered persons becomes an important source of status for their protectors' (Papanek, 1973, p. 317). Yet the very factors of male pride, purity of descent and tribal integrity are themselves rooted in ambivalence: women are seen as both guaranteeing the purity of descent and polluting it, as embodying the honour of the group and threatening it. The modesty code rests on two contradictory assumptions: that the woman is weak and needs to be protected from threats to her honour, and that she has strong sexual impulses which threaten the honour of the male and the integration of the group.[25] Perhaps the modesty code in Arab culture can be better understood in the light of such fundamental ambiguities.[26] The veil is a double shield, protecting the woman against external offences of society and protecting society against the inherent evil of woman. It has been argued that, because of a combination of biological and social factors, all cultures see woman as occupying a position on the boundary between culture and nature, belonging fully to neither one nor the other, and often fulfilling a role of mediation (Ortner, 1974). Perhaps the veil should be seen as a symbolic reminder of woman's liminal, and hence equivocal, dangerous and sacred status in society, as well as an attempt to neutralise the anxiety arising from contact with the sacred. 'The symbolism of the veil, then, belongs to the realm of the sacred in social relations' (Murphy, 1964, pp. 1270-1). It represents — and conceals — contradictions which lie at the core of all cultures: purity and pollution, good and evil, strength and weakness, communication and alienation. More generally, it symbolises the boundary between that which belongs to culture and that which is beyond it.

IV. Woman's Power in Society

In classical anthropological studies, patrilineal systems are defined by the positions and actions of men in groups, while women are seen as circulating between these groups. The commonly held — and erroneous — assumption is that women by being married off into groups are little more than items of exchange and can have no positive influence on the power structure of society.

In the case of Yemen, this view of the position of women could be supported by some aspects of marriage patterns. Generally, girls are married around the age of thirteen and are not consulted on the matter. The data of my fieldwork concur with a study of 169 San'ani women in which it was found that 105 women, or 62 per cent, had married between the ages of eleven and fifteen, and 20 per cent between the ages of fifteen and twenty (Chelhod, 1973a, 60-1). The results of another study show an average age at marriage of between thirteen and fourteen (Bornstein, 1974). Girls usually have little say in the planning of their marriage. Almost all my married informants told me that they had not met their husbands before marriage.[27] Their experiences were similar: about a month before the date of the marriage, the girl's mother would tell her that she did not have to do housework. Then she would take her to the public bath.[28] When she learns that a marriage has been arranged for her, the girl becomes very sad but she has no way of changing her parents' decision.

Besides limitation by early marriage, freedom of choice is further restricted by the Islamic practice whereby a man may take up to four wives and has a unilateral right of divorce. There is little data on the actual frequency of polygyny and the rates of divorce. One study found the 'rapport de polygamie' to be 1.77; in other words, for the 289 husbands interviewed in the sample, there were 514 wives (Chelhod, 1973). As for divorce, the rate appears to be fairly high according to a United Nations report: out of a sample of 54 San'ani women, 13 per cent had been divorced once and 10 per cent twice.[29] My own observations indicated that women who, either directly, or through friends and relatives, have experienced divorce or polygyny, perceive these as crucial problems in their lives and as undesirable practices in Yemeni culture. The prospect of their husband taking another wife is a source of sadness for all women. One of my informants told me about a nightmare in which her husband had chosen a *ṭabīna* (co-wife) from among her friends. Another one said: 'If he gets another wife, I will push her into the oven!' And one girl whose younger sister was being bothersome said to her: 'I wish you would marry someone as a *ṭabīna* so that you suffer as much as you are making me suffer!' Another informant had agreed to marry a man on the basis of his promise to divorce his first wife. Then he refused to do so and as a result she experienced two years of an unhappy marriage, marked by constant conflict with the first wife. (Ultimately, she sought and obtained a divorce.)

Early marriage, divorce and polygyny, the restrictions which they represent and the conflicts they cause for the women would thus support the idea of a male-dominated society. However, there are other aspects of marriage practices which draw attention to the possibilities for women to manipulate situations to their own advantage. First, it should be noted that some women find themselves in a position to decide about their marriage. Divorcees, widows and orphans, having been partially freed of the ties that constrain most women, can more easily accept or reject a suitor. The divorced women I interviewed were all very definite about wanting to choose their next husband and about getting to know him beforehand, or not marrying again at all. The relative freedom connected with a girl's second marriage is the point of the Yemeni proverb which goes: 'Your first marriage is made by your parents, the second by yourself.' Another situation which permits some degree of personal choice in marriage is that of the fatherless household. Among my informants, out of ten unmarried girls who were strongly in favour of deciding about their own marriage, six were girls whose father was deceased. One of them staunchly rejected all suitors saying she did not wish to get married for she had seen enough of the problems of marriage. She said that her mother would not force her because girls whose father is deceased might do as they please. Another girl kept changing her mind about whom she wished to marry. She had first been engaged to one boy but later decided she did not like his appearance anymore, then became engaged to another boy, whom she decided to leave, and finally married in a traditional way her paternal cousin (*ibn 'amm*). Thus, within the limits of traditional marriage practices, there are certain situations where a girl can exercise some choice about her marriage plans.

In general however, the female does not seem to have any 'positive choice' about whether or not to marry, and with whom.[30] On the other hand, she can force her husband to divorce her, and thus gain at least some 'negative choice', in breaking a marriage she no longer wants. In other words, the right to divorce may be the male's privilege, but the power to get a divorce is just as much in the hands of the woman. It is significant that of the eight cases of divorced women I studied, six had actively sought the divorce themselves and convinced their fathers or brothers to contact the religious judge (*qādi*). There are legally defined circumstances under which a female can get a divorce by having recourse to a *sharī'a* court: among these are the inability of her husband to support her economically, his failure to do justice to co-wives, mental disorders and physical defects such as impotency. Those of my informants who wanted a divorce used these legal stipulations to realise their aim. One of them even succeeded in getting a divorce while her case did not exactly fit the legal requirements. Her husband, she told me, for no apparent reason, and while she was visiting her mother, had written the first 'I divorce thee' paper. When asked why he did it, he replied it was *lil 'adab*, to 'teach' her (who is the boss). Since she had been forced to marry him, and had been having trouble with his family, she decided to go ahead and complete the divorce process. She convinced her brother to help with the court case. 'What if he decided to "teach me" ', she said, 'and I happened to be pregnant or had a baby?' She won the case, thus reversing the situation to her own advantage.

Moreover, when a man, for whatever reason, divorces his wife, other women may still express the cause of the divorce in terms of the attributes and behaviour of the wife rather than the whims of the husband. Gossip and rumour may then be used to present the social reality as the women choose to see it. I was once inquiring about why one tribal *shaikh* had divorced his third wife. One woman answered, 'Because that woman was dirty.' As to why he had married his fourth wife, another woman said, 'Because she was pretty and she knew how to attract him.' Another added: 'But will she know how to keep him?' Now, certainly there are political reasons behind the divorce and the marriage of this *shaikh*, but it is significant that the establishment and breaking of alliances is expressed by women in terms of women's qualities and behaviour. Women thus do not seem to see themselves as pawns that men move around, but as active participants in the system of marriage relations.

Patterns of seclusion also contribute in an unexpected way to give women more decision-making power; since men cannot know girls outside the immediate kin group, they are completely dependent upon their female relatives for advice.[31] Women can influence their brothers and sons by controlling the circulation of information about other females through gossip, through access to the reports of children who run errands and hear things from their playmates, and, most importantly, through visiting. Women are conscious of the importance of *tafriṭa* for planning future marriages. One mother expressed this by saying: 'I do not take my daughter to *tafriṭa* yet, it is too early for her to get married.' Another one told me about her brother's wife, and said explicitly, 'We saw her and wanted her for our brother' — a very clear affirmation of the women's part in making the choice. Fayein has noted the same attitude among the women she encountered:

Actually, the marriages are arranged by the women, though superficially it is the father who makes the decision. A young man attaches more importance to his mother's and his sisters' advice, for they are the only ones who know his proposed bride-to-be. On the wedding day, when he raises the veil which covers her, she is almost always a discovery for him, whereas the girl, when she opens her eyes, does not see a stranger before her. The women maintain a solid front in regard to the masculine world, and the fiancée will have been shown her future husband from behind a door or a closed window-blind. Perhaps she will have heard the sound of his voice as he climbs the stairs crying, 'Allah!' and even, if he has already been married, she will have learned all the details of his private life from harem gossip. (Fayein, 1957, p. 96)

Both by planning and plotting other people's marriages, and by being able to break their own — or even others' — marriages, women gain some power over the system of alliances that keeps society together.[32] The political importance of women as 'knots' in the social system has been recognised by Peters in his study of Cyrenaican tribal society:

The pivotal points in any field of power in this, a superficially dominant patrilineal, patrilocal and patriarchal society where the male ethos is vulgar in its brash prominence, are the women. What holds men together, what knots the cords of alliances are not men themselves, but the women who depart from their natal household to take up residence elswhere with a man, and who, in this critical position communicate one group to another. (1966, p. 15)

Friedl also points out than in kinship-based societies, it is the private sphere which is crucial for understanding the distribution of power in society:

There may be many cultures in which male activity is accorded pre-eminence in the public sector. But if a careful analysis of the life of the community shows that, pragmatically, the family is the most significant unit, then the private and not the public sector is the sphere in which the relative distribution of power to males and females is of the greatest importance. (1967, p. 97)

In other words, one may argue that women, by having control over the private domain of social life, may enjoy a certain amount of power. We thus would find ourselves confronted with two apparently contradictory images of women's status.

On the one hand, it is true that women's freedom of movement is greatly limited, that their activities are confined to
the home, that they are forced into early marriages with men
they do not know and that they have no real authority in the
public sphere of decision-making; however, on the other hand,
it is also true that men are excluded from the world of
women, cannot decide about their own marriages without
women's advice, and that women can and do influence
decision-making and seem to be aware of the possibility for
them to manipulate others and exercise power.[33] To gain a
better understanding of this problem, one would need some
rethinking and research on the relationship between public
and private spheres of decision-making, and, more importantly, on the changing relation between the public and the
private in a transitional society. This will not be attempted
here.[34] What we have tried to do is merely point out that the
reality of women's status and power is a 'multidimensional'
one, and that there may be more than one approach to studying it.

V. Ritual and Symbolism

The line of thought followed thus far leads us to consider the
possibility that two opposed aspects of reality coexist and are
intertwined in San'ani social life. We can define as the 'male
dominance' model of society that set of facts and ideas which
seem to support the notion that somehow or other men are
most important both politically and morally, that they control decision-making, and are the locus of cultural value. This
'male' model usually takes priority because it is expressed
historically in the politics and ideology of Yemeni culture.
One may argue that, in many cultures, the male view of the
world is a 'surface structure', and that a consideration of the
deeper levels of the culture will often reveal an autonomous
female view. Symbolic structures such as myths make statements that conflict with objective measures of economic or
political status. 'The study of symbolism uncovers certain
valuations of women — some of which make more sense if
women, not men, had made them (they conflict with the
social models of men)' (Ardener, 1973, pp. 140-1).
    It is necessary to make clear that male and female models

do not refer to separate realities but project images of the same reality. Even within a single individual, these images may coexist and constitute alternatives for defining social reality and acting within it. Perhaps the best way to grasp the female dimension of reality is through an interpretation of the central rituals of female society.

According to Leach, ritual is not a specific type of social action, but the expressive or 'technically superfluous' aspect of all social action. Here we shall use the term ritual to refer to those actions that are predominantly aesthetic, technically non-functional, as opposed to those that are predominantly profane, technical, functional. And if 'ritual is a symbolic statement which says something about the individuals in the action', as well as about the social order in general (Leach, 1965, pp. 12-14), what kinds of statements are made in the feminine rituals of San'ani culture?

In the preceding pages, we discussed the female separate sphere and suggested that when women talk about themselves, they do not seem to think in terms of men being superior and more important, and women being inferior, powerless and submissive. The perception of society by women does not necessarily conform to the male model. Our analysis of *tafriṭa* as the central ritual in women's daily life shows that the care with which women adorn themselves in the absence of men, the dancing and music, the absence of the veil and the strict exclusion of men from these gatherings all combine to confirm the community of participants over against the rest of (male) society.

A deeper consideration of the other 'symbolic statements' made during the various types of afternoon visits is even more revealing. Thus, if one examines the content of the stories and jokes that are told during these visits, it becomes obvious that the image of men implied in them contradicts the cultural ideals of manhood. Some stories are about the relations between men and women, and describe men as being fooled by women who are much more cunning and clever. One such story concludes with the male character saying 'I thought I knew all of the tricks of women, but I had assumed too much on my part.' Often during these visits women joke about men generally and even parody their behaviour. One of my informants once entered the sitting room (*mafrij*) wearing her father's white robe and imitated the pretentious way in which men act amongst themselves, provoking laughter and satisfaction from her audience. The same disrespect for the ideals of the male world is expressed in parts of the marriage *tafriṭa* where the women sing songs that are a bizarre imitation of *ghazal* (a genre of Arabic love poetry), and in which the attributes of men are described by comparing them with quite prosaic things. The general tone is one of satire and ridicule towards males, and the image of sexual relations expressed in them has very little to do with the ideals of the married state.[35] Fayein describes some satirical plays that are performed at marriage *tafriṭa*, and they all make fun of men and their ideals.

> The evening spent by the women was often full of gusto. Old women served as entertainers, and some of them were very popular. Their services had to be booked far in advance, and were rewarded with little gifts. I saw one of them display amazing acting ability. Disguised as a man and assisted by a leading lady, she played several satirical scenes of masculine life: first, that of a man who slaughtered a sheep and wished to give the best of the meat to his sweetheart, but was too carefully watched by his wife; then that of the man who wished to go to Mecca to have a good time, but whose wife made a frightful row; then that of the man who had been to Mecca and was trying to teach his friends how to pray. This last was played with a totally disrespectful realism. Just as he prostrated himself with his head lower than his rump, he let fly vulgar noise. (1957, p. 191)

These farces not only poke fun at the men, which is a rather obvious point, but at a deeper level they treat all society with ridicule and scorn, and especially the public sector of religion and ritual dominated by the males.

Moreover, some of the traditional customs enacted at the marriage *tafriṭa* have an ambiguous significance. For instance, when the bride enters the house of the groom her friends and relatives break eggs on her passage; when she crosses the threshold, she places her foot on a *jambiya* (the curved dagger worn by all Yemeni males as a symbol of manhood); and at both marriage and birth *tafriṭa* participants carry a strong-smelling plant, the *shadhāb*, as a sign of joy. The surface explanation for these customs as given by some informants and adopted by observers (Chelhod, 1973, pp. 25-9) is that they are meant to bring good luck. Thus, breaking eggs would bring fertility, and stepping on a symbol of fighting and death (the dagger) would ward off evil spirits and bring peace. Such an interpretation would help explain the presence of eggs, but not why they have to be broken as part of the ritual; it explains why stepping on the *jambiya* can be seen as a triumph over potential conflicts, but not why it is the bride herself who has to perform the ritual; it does not explain why the *shadhāb* would be selected as a symbol of joy when it is a very simple-looking plant without flowers, commonly grown in every backyard. In other words, the 'good luck' explanations seem both partial, and at the same time a bit too obvious. At a deeper level of analysis, one may suggest a different interpretation.[36] One may argue that when eggs are broken, male ideas about fertility are treated with scorn; that by stepping on the *jambiya*, the girl is defiling the male symbol *par excellence*; that the presence of *shadhāb*, which in folk medicine is well-known for inducing abortions,[37] is a silent insult to men and their conception of marriage, and a warning signal that women have a final say in what concerns men most.[38]

Thus the contention is that in their 'separate rituals' women act in a way that is a blatant refutation of the ideals of the patriarchal system. In such a system, women are expected to accept their roles as good wives and mothers as ideals to live up to. A closer examination of the covert aspects of their 'subculture' shows that they can be less than enthusiastic about these ideals, and in fact, silently ridicule them. This interpretation as a hypothesis, can help us be aware that in Yemeni culture there are areas of the female world that are situated beyond, and may even be in contradiction with, the dominant ideals of the male world.

Notes

1. For an interesting discussion of women's second rank in most cultures, see Rosaldo, 1974.

2. *Qāt* (*catha edulis*) is a small shrub, the leaves of which are chewed to produce a state of mental alertness, wakefulness, and a pleasant stimulation of the senses. *Qāt* seems to be a non-addictive stimulant; its active ingredients are alkaloids of the amphetamine type. Though research on the medical aspects of *qāt* is insufficient, its side-effects include loss of appetite, gastritis and constipation. The custom of chewing *qāt* in the afternoon is the subject of much controversy, and has some violent opponents. Others compare it in prevalence and in function to the custom of cocktails in the West. For the social and ritual aspects of *qāt*, see G. Obermeyer, 1973.

3. *Qishr* is an infusion made from the husks of coffee beans, sugar and spices.

4. The etymology of the word *tafriṭa* is complex. The derived forms of the triliteral root *faraṭa* convey various and disparate meanings such as 'to precede people to a water well', to send someone as a messenger', 'to praise immoderately', 'to be remiss, lazy, indolent' (Lane's *Lexicon*, 1863-93). The form *tafarraṭa* which is used in San'a to mean 'to go to the afternoon visit', is not found in this sense in any lexicon. It is perhaps significant that we do not find a clear definition of the word *tafriṭa*, for the meaning of the ritual itself is ambiguous.

5. Of course, behind the manifest sociability are latent motives such as status display, status affirmation, the need for social drama and communal ritual.

6. Rosaldo (1974, p. 25) contrasts the 'vertical integration' of girls in an intergenerational world with the 'horizontal integration' of boys in competitive peer groups. This might be relevant here.

7. See Chodorow's interesting article (1974), which discusses the relation between family structure and the formation of femine personality.

8. In Zaidi Islam, Imams are accorded the right of complementing and amending some legal provisions, as long as they can justify their stand by referring to the Koran or the Hadith literature.

9. Both Chodorow (1973) and Maher (1974) point out the importance of all-female groups for economic co-operation and social support.

10. 'Even in patrilocal societies in which women's status is very low, women do not translate this cultural devaluation into low self-esteem' (Chodorow, 1974, p. 65).

11. It should be made clear here that this applies to urban women, not peasant or tribal women. The latter participate more directly in the production process and have much more work both at home and outside. By travelling around Yemen, I was able to observe the great differences between urban and rural women's lives. Peasant women work in the fields all year, tribal women take care of animals, process their skins, spin their wool. Almost all non-urban women have to fetch wood and water every day, have little leisure time, and generally, their life conditions are much more difficult and their existence much harsher.

12. Certainly, underneath the ritualised appearance of *tafriṭa*, the surface of smooth and easy interaction, are latent conflicts and rivalries. The daily visit, while fulfilling an integrative function may also constitute an arena for the emergence and expression of conflicts, especially in the context of a changing society.

13. The fact that the actions and thoughts of women do not conform to the male dominance model delimited by the political ideology, suggests, as Ardener (1973) has pointed out, that there may coexist a male and a female model of

society, the former dominant, the latter muted.
14. For a study of sex differences in speech patterns, see E. Keenan, 'Ins and Outs of Women's Speech', *Cambridge Anthropology*, Vol. 1, No. 3, April 1974.
15. This may be related to what Ardener (1973) refers to as the similarity in 'articulacy' between male informants and ethnographers, whereas women are seen as being relatively inarticulate in this respect.
16. Traditional San'ani houses are composed of several storeys with a staircase between them. The *mafrij*, where friends gather, is generally on the top floor.
17. When women walk in the streets, the only man that I ever saw them greet is the *qashshām* (or onion grower) who belongs to a very low social category, one where marriage can only be endogamous and status inherited – a caste then, by most definitions.
18. Similarly, it is only partially true to say that 'a woman in the world of men is seen as a trespasser. Her identity must therefore be hidden and her physical appearance veiled. She is required to exist incognito' (Hilal, 1971, p. 85).
19. See Papanek (1973) for a very perceptive article on veiling in Pakistan.
20. The category of men covered by the incest taboo is defined in the Korān, Sūra 24. (This Sūra is also one of the main references about veiling in the Korān).
21. The *akhdām* (literally, 'servants') are said to be descended from slaves. They differ from the rest of the population by a darker complexion and African or Abyssinian facial features, but their exact origin is unknown. (See T.J. Arnaud, 'Les Akhdam de l'Yémen, leur origine probable, leurs moeurs', *Journal Asiatique*, Avril 1850, série 4, vol, 15, pp. 376-87.) The *akhdām* live on the margin of San'ani society – both physically and socially. They have 'houses' on the fringes of the city, so low and wretched that to the outsider they look more like a heap of garbage than like houses. The *akhdām* 'specialise' in begging, streetsweeping and prostitution; their women are unveiled.
22. Papanek points out the correlation between 'purdah' (seclusion and veiling) and high social standing (1973, p. 297). Similarly, I am told that in Afghanistan only middle-class and upper-class women are veiled.
23. Weddings are celebrated separately – and differently – by men and by women. For the 'male side' of wedding ceremonies, see Chelhod, 'Les cérémonies de mariage au Yémen', *Objets et Mondes*, XII, 1973.
24. For a valuable discussion of the veil functioning to symbolise social distance, see Murphy's analysis of the use of the veil by men of the Tuareg tribe (1971).
25. The veil would thus exist in cultures where impulse control, rather than being internalised, is shifted to external social institutions (Papanek, 1973, p. 316).
26. One may also reconcile in this manner the divergent views expressed by Antoun and Abu-Zahra about the modesty of women in Arab Muslim villages (*American Anthropologist*, Vol. 70, No. 4, August 1968, and Vol. 72, No. 5, October 1970).
27. Fifteen out of my twenty married informants did not meet their husbands before marriage. This figure however is misleading because the five women who did know their husbands came from quite atypical families who had lived abroad for a long time and cannot be considered representative. In generalizing then, one may say that the proportion of women who do not meet their husband before marriage is higher than 75 per cent.
28. It may be that the practice of taking the girl to the *hammām* (public bath) before her marriage functions to allow the female relatives of the groom to make sure that the bride-to-be has no physical defects.
29. A. Bornstein, Food and Agriculture Organization Report, 1974. These

figures may be slightly higher than reality because the sample was selected from among women working at the textile factory of San'a which is known to employ a large number of divorced women.

30. From a judicial point of view, women's consent is inferred from her silence at the time the marriage contract is being signed. If she cries and screams however, the contract can be invalidated.

31. It seems that boys do not have much more to say about whether or not to get married than girls do. Several boys told me that their parents had forced them to get married. One of them added that they had threatened to stop supporting his studies financially if he refused. Moreover, I gathered from the confidences of girls that at marriage the boy seems as much, if not more, frightened than the girl.

32. One may even venture the suggestion that women have special power to control fertility in society as a consequence of seclusion. Yemen has a birth rate which is significantly lower than that of other underdeveloped countries in the area. This puzzling demographic fact might be explained by the possibility of frequent abortions or by other forms of control over fertility. In a society where the female sphere is to a great extent beyond the control of men, it would not be surprising to find out that women could form a coalition and help provide abortions without men's knowledge in cases of unwanted pregnancies.

33. Some authors have suggested a 'life-cycle approach' to the problem of women's superior or subordinate status, by which one considers the question from the developmental family cycle or the life history cycle point of view: 'In traditional societies, girls had an inferior position in youth but acquired great powers as heads of enlarged households in middle or later age: in our society, girls have great freedom of choice in youth but often feel unwanted and left behind when the children grow up' (Richards, 1974, p. 7).

34. Chapter 3, however, includes a discussion of the changing roles of women in relation to the public and private spheres of social life.

35. These rituals might resemble Gluckman's 'rituals of rebellion' where subordinates act out a drama of resentment of authority while at the same time lending it a kind of legitimacy. In the case of *tafriṭa* however, the 'drama' is not an extraordinary calendrical event but an everyday process, and therefore contributes to defining an autonomous sphere of meaning.

36. No claim is made that such an interpretation is the only one and can be substituted for all others. A Freudian explanation, for example, would undoubtedly be valid here.

37. This is based on interviews with nurses and doctors who had heard about the practice, as well as with women who had used *shadhāb* to induce abortions.

38. Yet another symbol present at the marriage *tafriṭa* can be interpreted in terms of an autonomous female model of society. It is a wooden stick with numerous strings attached to its top, and on each string are threaded various items; one will have several broken eggshells, another cigarette-ends, a third one discarded candy wrappers or torn pieces of cloth, another will have uncooked beans, yet another the fruits of a wild tree which are too bitter to eat. It is called a *ḥijab* and is hung in the reception room or passed around among the women amid laughter and satirical songs. It is interesting to note that the same word *ḥijab* is generally used to refer to cloth or silver containers of a verse from the Koran, which are hung around the neck, pinned on clothes or on the belt as a protection against evil. This may at first suggest another 'good luck' explanation, which again would only be superficial. In fact, all the items which are hung on the *ḥijab* have something in common: they are either 'too natural' or 'already consumed' and cannot be of any use in the realm of human culture. Thus uncooked beans and bitter fruit cannot be eaten, and eggshells, cigarette-ends and bits of paper or cloth are useless 'leftovers', the refuse of cultural activity. Moreover, unlike the other *ḥijab* which have religious connotations, this one is handled with laughter and disrespect – as if it were a 'mock-*ḥijab*'. In a way then, it can be viewed as an anti-symbol and a reminder of woman's limited status on the boundary between culture and non-culture.

2 MODERN FORCES

> We may view traditional societies
> with nostalgia or disgust: be enchanted
> by their beauty, or revolted by their
> cruelty. It doesn't matter: they no
> longer present a viable alternative.
> (Gellner, 1964)

I. Historical Background

The severe isolation of North Yemen in recent centuries has been partly due to its relative lack of importance for colonial powers, but it was also the result of the closed-door policy of its Zaidi rulers. Imams Yahya (1904-48) and Ahmed (1948-62) both had an adamant policy of keeping out foreigners as well as their modern innovations. The aim of the Imams was to keep the country free from foreign interference in order to preserve its independence and its traditional religious way of life — as well as their own power.

This policy, however, was not wholly feasible since Yemen was not economically self-sufficient and depended on other countries for numerous basic products. Private contacts for commercial business were necessary in the absence of a state economy and a number of Yemeni merchants established themselves outside the country. Also, the poverty of Yemen, especially the southern regions, as well as the oppressiveness of the regime, contributed to driving many Yemenis out to seek better life conditions in Aden, Ethiopia and elsewhere. Moreover, the Imams themselves found it necessary to establish relations with other countries, and, even though their motive was primarily to bolster their traditional regime through the purchase of arms and military equipment, they inadvertently introduced modern influences via the army. Those students who were sent to the military academies of other Arab countries, especially Iraq, as well as those whose families had sent them for an education abroad encountered more progressive ideas and were later to constitute one of the main forces of change in the country. In their efforts to increase their domination, the Imams developed mechanisms of communication and control, which, given the internal forces of change and endogenous pressures, were later to be used against the Imamate. However unwillingly, the last two Imams had contributed to generating change — and their own destruction.[1]

Under Imam Ahmed agreements were signed with foreign countries (including the USSR and China) for the construction of roads connecting the major cities, agricultural projects and a number of small industries. Table 2 shows that, already under the Imamate of Ahmed, small industries had slowly begun to increase. Moreover, medical missions (Russian, Chinese, Italian and French) began working at that time[2] and a number of development projects were in operation.

It would thus be inaccurate to say that modernising changes began only with the 1962 Revolution. Certain forces had been set to work before 1962 and were slowly transforming the traditional culture. The Revolution was the expression of many structural changes which had occurred much earlier. The various regimes since the time of the Revolution have couched their claims to power in terms of an ideology of national development. Each stated that its primary goal was the development of the country and compensation for the delay accumulated during the 'years of ignorance'.[3]

With a great deal of help from international agencies and other countries, Yemen is now attempting to deal with the obstacles that hinder its development: an underdeveloped economy, poor communications, bad health conditions, and a traditional education system. The United Nations accepted Yemen as a member in 1947, and established offices in San'a in 1970; in 1971 financial aid from the United Nations was $240 million, of which $86 million came from the United States. Yemen also receives aid from the USSR and socialist bloc to the amount of $103 million in 1972. The Arab countries (mostly Saudi Arabia, Egypt, Kuwait and the United Arab Emirates) contributed $56 million in 1972. Of the European countries, West Germany is the largest contributor ($33.5 million).[4]

The pace of change seems rapid and slow at the same time; rapid if we consider what has been accomplished in less than a decade, but extremely slow if we consider all that remains to be done. In the case of education, for example, between 1965 and 1970, the increase in primary school enrolment was of 10 per cent; while between 1970 and 1972 it was of 32 per cent. Yet in 1972, only 12 per cent of the eligible age groups were attending primary school, and only 1 per cent were attending secondary school. Girls currently represent 10 per cent of primary and 6 per cent of secondary school enrolment, and schoolgirls only 1.6 per cent of the age groups concerned.[5]

Tables 2-5 give an idea of the development of some sectors over the past few years.[6]

Table 2: Development of Industries in San'a, by Year of Starting Production (Includes Small Artisanal Industries)

Before		
1960 - 89		
1960 - 16	1966 - 25	1972 - 89
1961 - 11	1967 - 90	1973 - 94
1962 - 17	1968 - 19	
1963 - 15	1969 - 17	
1964 - 18	1970 - 49	
1965 - 20	1971 - 36	

Table 3: Population of San'a by Educational Level, 1973

Educational Level	Number	Per cent
Illiterate	61,705	67.22
Literate	13,255	14.44
Primary	12,475	13.59
Preparatory	2,075	2.25
Secondary	1,790	1.95
University	495	0.54
	91,795	100.00

Table 4: Development of Health Indicators in Yemen

	Physicians	Medical assistants	Hospitals	Beds	Dispensaries	Drug-stores
1968	150	616	22	3,450	5	108
1969	176	643	23	3,470	5	109
1970	184	643	26	3,670	5	118
1971	199	720	29	3,875	7	128
1972	203	720	31	3,905	9	129
1973	203	878	31	3,878	13	130
1975	182	747	28	3,317	9	—

Table 5: Development of Health Indicators in San'a, 1973

	Physicians	Medical assistants	Hospitals	Dispensaries
1968	80	195	5	3
1969	80	255	5	3
1970	80	267	5	3
1971	82	279	5	5
1972	83	279	5	5
1973	83	380	5	9

This brief sketch of the modernisation process at the national level is more meaningful if we narrow down our scope to consider how the various changes are experienced at the level of a San'ani woman's life. I asked my informants what had been, in their opinion, the major changes in the country since the Revolution.[7] There were, generally, two types of response. Some perceived modernity as a set of new facilities and objects for use within the home, others perceived it in terms of broader changes such as the provision of roads, hospitals and schools.

The practical and more obvious dimension of modernisation is for many women that which influences their perception of change. Thus, to the question 'What has changed in Yemen?' one woman replied: 'Before, they used pottery for cooking, now we use aluminium ware. Also, before, they dressed differently, now some girls wear *bantalōn* [modern trousers] under their dress.' Another woman said: 'Before, the bride used to wear the *tāj Yamani* [traditional Yemeni headcover], on the day of marriage, now many wear the *tāj masri* [Egyptian headcover, close to the Western type, and now prevalent in many Arab countries] '. A number of other women said the higher cost of living had been a major change, and gave examples of the increase in the price of various goods.

The world of the household reflects the material − and superficial − dimension of change in the life of women. The most common modern objects in a typical middle-class and upper-class San'ani house are: in the kitchen, a gas stove, which is added to but does not replace, the traditional *tannūr* (oven), as well as aluminium pots and pans; in the sitting-room, electric lamps hanging from the ceiling, pictures of family members and Indian movie actors hanging on the wall, side by side with the Korān in its traditional brocade purse, the radio and cassette-player (probably the most popular of all modern items[8]) and, since 1975 in some houses, a television set conspicuously enthroned in the middle of the room.

Thus, at the level of the household, what represents modernity is its more concrete aspects such as the cost of objects, and more importantly, the availability of new objects. 'Undeniable usefulness', says Berque about modern household items, 'but also facticity ... since they are only the indirect result of a modernization [that is passively] accepted or endured, rather than imposed by the males' (1969, p. 206). These objects, however factitious, are nevertheless one important medium through which women are 'tuned', both technically and symbolically, to the rest of the world. The symbolic significance of modern objects is apparent from people's attitudes towards them: modern electrical appliances especially are handled with conspicuous care, as one would handle a foreign, fragile, perhaps sacred thing. We may be dealing here with a subtle phenomenon related to a new symbolisation process about status and about change: in a very abstract sense, some of these objects are precious and even sacred because they represent what Gellner calls 'the magic of industrial society' to which only a few have access.

Beyond the household sphere, the perception of change seems directed towards three sectors: health facilities, education and the mass media. Here our focus is on the way in which the role and image of the woman are affected by, and in turn manifest, these changes. We have defined as agents of change those institutions which constitute new bases of association and provide alternatives — either in the form of social roles, or at the ideological level in the form of images and legitimations — to the familial roles and images to which women are traditionally confined. These agents of change include: the school, both primary and secondary where an increasing number of girls are enrolled; the San'a textile factory, founded by the Chinese in 1967 and which employs about 400 women; the offices of commercial companies which may hire women; the hospitals and dispensaries established by various medical missions which train and hire women as nurses; the nursing school; the Institute of Public Administration; and the newly started San'a University funded by Kuwait.[9]

Before discussing in the next chapter the effect of these institutions on the life of San'ani women, we will describe briefly two which explicitly define themselves as aiming at effecting changes in the lives of women. These are: The Woman's Association and the Family Radio Programme.

II. The Yemeni Woman's Association (*Jam'iyat al Mar'a al Yamaniya*)[10]

Four of the women I interviewed were active participants in the Woman's Association. By talking to them, visiting the office of the Association, as well as through the comments of those women who, while not involved in it, had some knowledge about it, one gets the impression that its impact has been uneven and limited.

The *Jam'iya*, or rather what was later to become the *Jam'iya*, already existed under the Imamate. At that time, some upper-class women used to gather and go to visit poor families to help them materially. With the overthrow of the Imamate, that charity institution was to regress and disappear. After the Revolution, some kind of association emerged, which formulated new aims in relation to the idea of woman's contribution to national development. But that association was active for only a short while and then almost non-existent. A great step was accomplished when a number of women who were holding important positions in society became involved in it: among these were the wife of the Prime Minister, the head of the nursing school, the first Yemeni female doctor, and the girl in charge of the Family Radio Programme. In 1974 the *Jam'iya* obtained some government support and set up a permanent office.

The aims of the Association were to deal with the problems of high illiteracy, insufficient knowledge about household and child care, early marriage and family problems. To cope with the first two of these problems courses were set up to teach adult women reading and writing, some elements of English as well as a few household skills. As for familial problems,[11] the *Jam'iya* used to present approximately once a week in the daily paper *Al Thawra* a special page where current familial problems were discussed. The articles would include discussions of the changing condition of the Yemeni girl, of teachers and their importance, of how to have a successful husband-wife relationship, of the mother-in-law and her role in divorce, and so on. Once in a while, on the woman's page, the particular problem of a reader was published with advice for its solution.

Few of the women I encountered ever talked about it or had had any contact with it; still fewer were involved in it. Moreover, the activities sponsored by the *Jam'iya* did not seem to be very popular: the woman's page in *Al Thawra* could only influence a very small number of women, given illiteracy rates; and, the office of the Association, where I expected to find many women involved in various activities, did not seem to be dynamic. In spite of the enthusiasm and commitment of the members, the Association did not have the success which might be expected. This fact is all the more puzzling since in a society where women are illiterate and restricted to the home, one would anticipate that the opportunities for change provided by an institution like the *Jam'iya* would be most welcome.

One partial reason for this has to do with the fact that at the time of fieldwork, the Association was apparently going through one of its 'low' phases because its president, being pregnant, could not devote as much time to it as she used to; hence, the slowing down of all activities, a situation of which other members were aware and which they discussed. The Association was precarious since it was dependent upon persons rather than institutionalised offices and routinised activities. Another reason which was put forth by one of the old members of the *Jam'iya* explained the limited influence of the Association in terms of the attitude of women and their unwillingness to make an effort because of their expectation that everything should be 'served' to them. This explanation is interesting in that it expresses a fundamental difference in attitude: whereas the members of the *Jam'iya* are convinced that every woman should make an effort to change her condition, the 'average' uneducated woman does not feel the desire to change her condition and hence does not see the need for directing her energies towards this goal. But, behind this apparent indifference of women, there are deep social reasons, some structural, others ideological.

The former are related to the *Jam'iya* as a social group over against traditional social groupings. What in other cultures may constitute a major incentive for women to join a women's association, namely the opportunity to meet, discuss and pursue common activities in the context of an all-female group, is already present in traditional San'ani culture where women spend most of their lives, both work and leisure time, in all-female groups. From that point of view then, the *Jam'iya* does not offer something that the women would need but could not find in traditional society. In fact, women seem to prefer those groups where they can meet their friends and relatives to the more anonymous *Jam'iya*, all the more so as the notion of a voluntary association with clearly defined membership and activities is still foreign to the usual patterns of relations among women, which are generally diffuse and based on either kinship or neighbourhood.

More importantly, perhaps, the Association has not yet been able to formulate its aims in terms that are relevant to individual women: the value of literacy and education seem basic and obvious from the point of view of the society at large, but it is not self-evident to the individual uneducated woman who has lived most of her life without it and sees all her friends and relatives in the same situation. In other words, the prevailing cultural ideology is such that women do not have sufficient motives for joining the *Jam'iya*. Generally, those who already are convinced of the necessity to improve their status are not the ones who would most need the Association; whereas those who would benefit from its activities are precisely those who, because they have not been exposed to certain currrents of ideas, do not feel the desire to change their condition. Joining the *Jam'iya* implies that a conversion in one's world view has already taken place and it in turn entails a substantial transformation in one's life style. One may thus say that the Woman's Association requires too much from both the practical and ideological points of view without providing directly relevant incentives for individuals to join it. It therefore tends to remain for the time being restricted in its membership. This judgement about the *Jam'iya* should not imply it is not generating any change in San'ani society: it is an opportunity for women to meet, discuss relevant social problems and attempt to deal with them, which represents a definite change. The point is, however, that from the point of view of the 'average' San'ani woman, the *Jam'iya* in its present form, and given the cultural realities, is having a limited impact: the impetus for change where it exists is more often given by other institutions and through other channels. When I returned to San'a in 1976, I found that my 1974 impressions about the *Jam'iya* were verified: the Association was once again almost nonexistent, its president abroad, its office closed.

III. The Family Radio Programme (*Rukn al'Usra*)[12]

Less ambitious in its scope but more directly influential on the women's lives is the Family Radio Programme. It is broadcast for an hour daily, the morning half-hour session being repeated in the evening for those who do not have a chance to listen to it earlier. The programme typically includes: an informal lecture in simple terms about a relevant family topic or a current issue, a short play in typical San'ani language about some social problem, the presentation (in anonymous form) of a particular problem concerning one of the listeners with the advised solution for it, and finally, messages from listeners to their friends and relatives, congratulating them on a birth, marriage, or expressing their best wishes on special occasions.

The subjects dealt with in the programme include, for instance: the necessity of caring for the cleanliness of children, on the negative effects of *qāt*-chewing upon the family, on how to achieve a good relationship with one's husband, on how to deal with mothers-in-law, and on the possible effects of the limitation of *mahr* upon polygyny.[13]

Generally speaking, the Family Radio Programme is very popular. Most of my informants listened to it regularly, and all knew about it and had listened to it more than once. Women sometimes discussed it at afternoon visits, and, if some thought that it was naive and portrayed Yemenis as backward people,[14] the majority of my informants said that they liked it. Even men listened to it quite often and the girl in charge of the programme told me that it was under the pressure of male listeners that the programme, which was earlier called *Rukn al Mar'a* ('Woman's Corner'), was renamed *Rukn al'Usra* ('The Family Corner'): men could not afford to admit that they listened to a woman's programme, she said.

The popularity of *Rukn al'Usra* is a function of both its intrinsic qualities and its cultural context. As a daily programme it is cleverly done and succeeds in being both instructive and entertaining, where music alternates with didactic parts, plays and the 'social page'. No effort is needed to understand even the educative parts because abstract ideas are always clarified and illustrated by examples or by a play. It does not require any break in the woman's life, since she can listen to it while doing housework. In this it differs from the Woman's Association which demands a more drastic change in daily schedule. Also, the programme does not aim at a radical transformation of the woman but attempts to achieve a gradual educational process. Through it the 'average' women is tuned to the outside world without having to leave the private world of the home. Whereas the Woman's Association attempts to get the woman out into the world, the Family Programme brings the outside world into the home. In that respect, it is better able to effect a junction between tradition and modernity. The programme visibly emerges from a constant interaction between the people producing it and the audience: most topics of discussion and subjects of plays are inspired by the written questions of listeners, by current events taking place in San'ani society, and by what the girl who directs the programme feels are relevant social problems.

Moreover, the programme provides a means of communication between listeners who may send messages to one another, hear about what women in their own society are doing and what kinds of problems are confronting other people. Through the programme, a kind of community is formed in which individuals, though they may not know one another, actually or potentially share the same problems and attempt to solve them with reference to similar standards. Thus, there emerges a certain awareness that each woman's problems are not unique, but may be common to other though unknown women, that individual problems can be interesting to the group (a group that is not the traditional kinship one), and that general issues are a direct concern of individuals. In other words, the particularistic approach to social relations and conflicts is gradually replaced by a universalistic one, and this constitutes one of the main factors in modernisation.

IV. Some Notes on Television

Since 1975, television has been, like everywhere else in the world, a dramatic force for change in Yemen. The impact of television on San'ani society is tremendous and it is a most interesting project to try and understand the many ways in which it is affecting traditional roles, aspirations, norms and values in a society which until two decades ago was living in almost complete isolation from the rest of the world. Here I will only suggest a few aspects of the effect of television on the women's lives, based on observations and interviews collected in 1976.

First, television constitutes a form of entertainment that is beginning to change the daily routine and to compete with traditional leisure patterns. People now tend to sleep much later in the evening than before, and sometimes prefer to stay at home and watch television instead of going visiting. In fact there is a conscious attempt, on the part of the government, to schedule the more popular programmes on the days and times where visiting is most intense, with the aim of substituting television for the *qāt* session and thus fighting the supposed detrimental effects of *qāt*. This policy, coupled with the erosion of the dramatic character of the afternoon visit (discussed in the next chapter), and the attractiveness of television as theatrical performance, may well undermine traditional visiting.

Moreover, unlike the afternoon visit, watching television is not a communal ritual, an 'organic' reality. It is patterned, not by personal relations among participants, but by the more mechanical relation between each individual and the source of messages. In this sense it is a new type of social experience, one which contributes to changing the quality of social relations. This change is especially striking in the case of the relations between the sexes. By projecting pictures of situations marked by the absence of seclusion and the free intermingling of the sexes, television is providing images that may come to constitute alternatives to traditional norms. This intrusion of television into the *ḥaram* of women's separate sphere is best illustrated by an anecdote. A number of my San'ani friends told me that some women who were watching television for the first time were caught by surprise at the appearance of the male newscaster and hurriedly veiled. Perhaps it is that the traditional television viewer is unable at first to appreciate the social distance implied by the screen: she must learn the boundary between impersonal and personal interaction, abstract and concrete encounters, in other words the bases of social relations in modern situations.

At the same time as they learn to 'translate' social relations, television viewers project themselves into the roles of other individuals and learn to perceive or experience the kinds of emotions described in the programmes which they watch. I have often listened to my San'ani friends relating with great sympathy and emotion, the tribulations of the heroine of last night's show. I have heard television viewers tell their friends who do not yet own a television set about the marvel-lous stories which they follow; I have sometimes noticed the exchange of glances and smiles about some episodes of love and passion, and I generally have formed the impression that love and happiness were becoming concerns of everyday life, or at least matter for dreaming.

More generally, television contributes to making the tradi-tional universe a reality which is not inevitable or necessary. Cultural phenomena from all over the Arab world and from Europe and America are projected into the home of the average San'ani and conjure up visions of alternatives to traditional ways of life. Paradoxically, this reveals the con-tingency of social arrangements, yet at the same time it pro-vides models to emulate and standards for achievement. Whereas in a traditional society discrepant realities are taken for granted, segregated and not allowed to shake the security of the traditional universe, in a transitional situation and with increased contacts it becomes impossible to contain the 'differences' and they are transformed into conflicts — which are most often resolved to the detriment of tradition.

Notes

1. For a more complete understanding of political transformations in Yemen see G. Obermeyer, *Messengers and Warriors: Center and Periphery Politics in South Arabia.* (Forthcoming.)

2. Fayein (1957) gives a vivid description of her life as a working doctor under the Imamate.

3. A number of informants, male and female, refer to the pre-Revolution years by the expresssion *kāna al jahl mukhayyam* ('Ignorance was prevalent').

4. The figures for foreign aid are from A. Saint-Hilare, 1975.

5. These statistics are taken from a United Nations Development Project aimed at improving the educational system, written in 1973.

6. All figures are from Central Planning Organisation, *Statistical Book*, 1973 and 1976. I have omitted some years where comparative figures were not available.

7. The significance of the Revolution as a turning point in the lives of women is manifested in part by the fact that women talk about various past events and count their ages and those of siblings or children with reference to the year of the *thawra* (revolution). In other words, the Revolution and its consequences are part of the 'subjective time' of all women.

8. The popularity of the radio and cassette-player is related to the cultural inclination of Yemenis towards music; this new object makes accessible to a large number of people what had for a long time been the privilege of an elite: hiring

a professional singer to entertain guests during visits.

9. The University had only three female students when it opened in 1970-1, about 125 in 1973-4, and about 300 in 1976.

10. Most of the discussion of the *Jam'iya* in this chapter is based on data gathered in 1974.

11. Another association related to the *Jam'iyat al Mar'a al Yamaniya* has begun to operate in the field of family problems: this is the *Jam'iyat Tanzim al 'Usra* which includes several of the members of the Woman's Association.

12. Before 1974 this programme was called *rukn al mar'a* (the woman's corner); in 1976, the name was changed again to *ṣuwar minal waqi'* (images from reality). But the form and content have remained almost the same throughout.

13. During the time of my fieldwork, in 1974, the government issued a decree limiting the maximum amount of money a father could ask as a bride price (*mahr*) for his daughter. A couple of days later, the programme presented a play in which a woman was worried that her husband would take a second wife now that *mahr* was lower. The moral of the story was that so long as a woman satisfies her husband and has a good relationship with him, he would not want another wife.

14. This opinion may be related to the fact that the programme addresses itself to the 'average' uneducated person and consequently simplifies arguments and explanations. It may also be a result of the very conception of the programme, which attempts to find the answers to specific problems. The person responsible for the programme herself admitted to me that her suggested solutions are always middle-of-the-road, because, she said, a strong above-average person could solve her own problems by herself and would not ask a stranger for advice. For these reasons the programme is not appreciated by a minority. In the future, and with the increase of education, it may have to reformulate its aims in relation to its changing audience.

3 JOURNEYS TO PUBLIC SPHERES

'And here I am, behind my cloak
An ardent hope and a burning fever
I thirst for meeting with you,
   my beloved
But there is my veil, my curse,
   O my beloved.'

(M. al Sharafī, 1970)

I. From Kinship to Friendship

The institutions that emerge in relation to the development
of health, education and mass communication services in
Yemeni society come to constitute the bases for the confrontation between old and new, and define the conditions
for the emergence of an alternative social world. The new
social groupings that become significant for modernising
women share certain characteristics which differentiate them
from traditional social groupings. They are situated outside
the home and are not defined by kinship criteria; the woman's
role within them is not an ascribed familial role, and her
status is relatively independent of her father's or husband's
social position. Thus, the women employed in the San'a
textile factory, and in commercial businesses are assigned
their jobs largely on the basis of their skills and capacities.
They are able to enter into relations with other women co-
workers, with superiors and subordinates and sometimes also
with foreign and Yemeni social workers. As in other Middle
Eastern countries,[1] many of the employed women especially
in factory work are divorced. At first glance, this would
suggest that divorced women were obliged to seek support
for themselves and that they could not rely on their family.
Even though this may be true to a certain extent, in many
cases, rather than being forced into working, divorced women
are to some extent free of those traditional constraints which
restrict women. They are not completely under the authority
of their fathers, and have been freed by divorce from their

65

husbands' authority. Yet according to *sharī'a*, the father of the divorced woman has the legal duty to support her until she marries again — if she wishes to do so — and to support her children until they reach the legally specified age when they return to their father. One may argue that a divorced woman can choose to take a job to supplement her family's income or her own but does not have to do so. In many cases she still can take advantage of her extended family and leave her children with her mother or another older female relative. Most of my informants who were divorced and had taken a job did in fact leave their children with their mother and only saw them outside working hours. Taking a job and leaving one's children at home or at a nursery[2] constitute new options superimposed upon traditional ones, and among which the individual may choose.

In the same way, medical facilities provide new alternatives for knowledge and social interaction. They bring women into contact with a wide range of people. It is the Yemeni mother who takes the children to the clinic, and there she interacts with specialists (doctors and nurses) as well as with other women, some friends and some strangers, who have similar problems. They also acquire new knowledge about a sector of life which they share with others outside the home. All women attempt to understand medical treatments and tend to follow the innovations in this field. A number of times I observed women exchanging information about new drugs and giving advice to one another, or trying to explain sickness in terms of their recently acquired knowledge. Modern institutions thus provide the context for new types of social encounters and interaction that do not refer to ascribed kin roles.

In the school, girls begin for the first time to build relationships outside the context of kinship, to share ideas referring to extra-domestic spheres of knowledge, and to derive pleasure from social relations which can only be described as individualistic and creative. One of my informants once showed me a notebook in which her friends from school had written various statements and wishes about life and friendship in the romantic idiom which is typical of schoolgirls in other parts of the Arab world. In traditional Yemeni culture, the theme of friendship appears in many songs, but it is restricted to relations between males and is expressed in a rather conventional manner. Traditionally, girls grow up with women of all ages and do not have a chance to forge bonds in the context of peer groups. The emergence of friendship between girls and the romantic expression of individual attachments are new phenomena. They indicate a change of focus from the realm of kinship to the 'other-than-kin' world and an expansion of social ties beyond the traditional sphere.

The 'other-than-kin' world may also come to include people who are outsiders not only to the world of kin but also to the culture. Because of the need of Yemen for trained personnel, a substantial number of non-Yemenis are actively involved in various development projects. For instance, a government report[3] indicates that in 1972-3, 92 of the 203 physicians working in Yemen, or 45 per cent, were non-Yemenis.[4] In 1975, the proportion of foreign physicians, nurses and qualfied midwives was 43 per cent. The number of foreign teachers is also significant: 884 out of a total of 4,688, or about 20 per cent in 1973;[5] in 1974, 1,166 out of 5,682 teachers were non-Yemenis, and 1,278 out of 6,889 in 1975 — a proportion of about 18 per cent. Doctors and teachers, as well as other foreign specialists, are in contact with traditional culture only in so far as they are experts in a certain field; they are not entangled in the web of primary relations in which Yemenis are involved. Interaction with them is restricted to the performance of those activities that are defined by the specialised situation and is often limited by the fact that they know just enough Arabic to go about their regular activities. Remaining to some extent outside the traditional complex of relations, they contribute to socialising the Yemenis with whom they come into contact into those institutions where interaction is structured according to well-defined role-sets rather than diffuse traditional ties.

But it is in the relations between the sexes that changes are most revealing. The school, the office and the university allow girls to have regular encounters with males not covered by the incest taboo and to discuss a variety of topics with them. Even though schools are not mixed, there may be a male teacher in a girls' school and the schoolgirls I have talked to said that a number of girls do not veil in class. The San'a University is mixed, and although all the Yemeni female students remain veiled, one can sometimes see incongruous scenes of a veiled girl carrying notebooks chatting with a group of male students, or sitting at a table with boys having a coffee break, or even being given a ride home by a relative or perhaps a friend. Women who are employed in commercial offices wear the *lithma* (inner veil) when there are men around, but take it off when working alone in an office. On the surface, this does not seem to depart from traditional practices in any way. Yet it implies a constant alternation of 'veil and no-veil' according to the fluctuating definition of the situation. By being repeated too often, this little performance is routinised and the ritual which marked all male-female encounters comes to lose its dramatic character.

Similarly, whereas playful infringements of veiling practices do not at first radically challenge the norm and are not sanctioned severely, frequent breaches and manipulations, even if minor, may over time result in altogether changing the pattern. Today in San'a more and more girls lift their veil in the street under various circumstances and pretexts, or walk with the black *khunna* completely lifted, their face covered only by the *lithma*. Thus it seems that, through a process of gradual erosion, the norms of veiling are changing and other alternatives eventually appear. In the cities of Yemen, a new type of outdoor garment is now being used and is slowly replacing the *sharshaf* and *sitāra*; this is the *bālṭo* (an adaptation of the Russian word for coat), a long-sleeved ankle-length coat worn over trousers, and with a scarf on the head. Even traditional San'anis concede that in theory, the *bālṭo* is in conformity with the requirements of modesty (as two authors agreed in the debate about the veil in the newspaper *Al Thawra*). For an increasing number of males and females, the *bālṭo* is considered an acceptable female dress.

Underlying the decreasing relevance of the veil is an important factor. In the school, the hospital, the office, the university, the individual woman is not seen as a 'generalised female' but as the occupant of a particular role which can be relatively independent of her traditional sex role. In other words, sex no longer permeates all male-female encounters but rather becomes one element in a relationship, and one which may, temporarily if not definitively, be bracketed and put aside. It becomes possible in principle to separate the components of an individual's status and to base a relationship upon those components that are directly relevant to the particular situation. Since part of the rationale of the veil is that it is a protective device separating 'mankind' from 'womankind', the emergence of role-specific relations between the sexes is bound to make it lose some importance.

This break with traditional practices between the sexes is not accepted by everyone and there are attempts to discourage parents from educating their daughters by circulating rumours against schoolgirls. One such rumour was that once girls start going to school, they become perverted and begin to use contraceptives. One girl also told me that the opposition to girls' education was so strong, especially from such groups as the *Ikhwān al Muslimīn* that the then Prime Minister had, on one important occasion, given a speech refuting all rumours and encouraging parents to educate their daughters. Still, conservative attitudes towards girls' education are reflected in the relatively high dropout rate for girls (78 per cent in 1972-3, United Nations, 1973). A number of girls did in fact complain to me that their parents had forced them to leave school even before they completed their primary education, and even though they wished to pursue their studies. Some parents may be afraid that too much education could jeopardise their daughters' chances of a good marriage. Nevertheless, more people seem to accept or take for granted that girls should to go school, and the increase in the number of girls enrolled at the university is an indication that things have begun to change, however slowly.

The new approach to male-female relations has been expressed by one of my informants in terms that deserve special attention because they reveal one of the mechanisms through which traditional patterns are changed, and new patterns 'grafted upon' tradition. That informant, a thirteen-year-old girl, asked whether she veiled in class when the teacher was a male, replied: 'He is like my brother, why should I veil in his presence?'

Such a statement is significant in more than one sense, the most obvious being that, as in many other cultures, the idiom of kinship is used to express the content of a non-kin relationship. At another level, it represents an interesting change in the approach to social relations. Traditional thinking sees all male-female encounters as potential sexual encounters, except in some well-defined cases such as those covered by the incest taboo. Hence the elaborate modesty code and its restrictions on behaviour. It is in this traditional idiom that the informant expressed the modern notion that it is possible for a male and a female to interact in terms of a relation not determined solely by sex. To the idea of sex as a diffuse element pervading all relations in society is thus opposed the idea of separating the components of one status on the basis of a specific role-set.

The statement discussed above is interesting in yet another respect. It expresses how, through the idiom of kinship, a role which in its modern form is foreign to Yemeni culture, comes to be incorporated in the traditional system: the teacher is like a brother. A similar case was brought to my attention by the head of the nursing school, who said that most of the students call her 'mother'. The teacher and the head of the school are thus symbolically incorporated into the kinship sphere. As persons who 'fit' between two cultures, the old and the new, and stimulate acceptance of new ideas and patterns, they may be seen as cultural brokers. People may relate to them in the traditional idiom even though they are active agents of change. The ambivalence which allows the cultural broker to operate on two levels, and even to manipulate both, is an expression of the constant dialectic between tradition and modernity. G. Obermeyer's case study of a cultural broker (1973a) emphasises the ability of the broker to understand tradition and empathise with traditional people even though he is consciously challenging the bases of the traditional political culture. This dual position is the root of the broker's power. The broker can manipulate traditional ties while being critical of tradition and attempting to change it. The role is a stimulus for change in that it can lead people into accepting modern patterns of behaviour which they would have otherwise refused. Thus, the head of the nursing school obtained permission from the parents of one of her students for their daughter to travel to Egypt. At first, the girl told me, her father was opposed to the idea because, he said, no unmarried girl travels by herself, but he was later convinced by the arguments of the head of the school who promised that she would take care of the girl as if she were her own daughter. In the traditional setting, the broker is capable of attaining a 'synthesis of nearness and distance',[6] nearness referring to involvement in traditional networks of relations, distance to the awareness of other opportunities and commitment to change.

The need to negotiate between tradition and modernity on the part of the broker becomes most dramatically apparent precisely in those cases where it is virtually impossible to achieve. A subtle example will help clarify this. School teachers, according to the accounts given to me by a Peace Corps teacher, often find themselves in a situation where the alternatives are either illicitly to give their class the examination questions ahead of time to 'help' the students pass easily, or refuse to do so. If they refuse they not only put their class at a disadvantage as compared with others (whose teachers may agree to 'prepare' their students), but also face the dislike and antipathy of their students. In other words, the dilemma is between being so 'close' as to compromise the rights and obligations of the teacher's role, or so 'distant' that communication with students becomes impossible. Cultural brokers thus find themselves at the juncture of two sometimes mutually exclusive options which they must attempt to reconcile. By using one to manipulate the other they consciously or unconsciously contribute to expanding the opportunities available to women, help them accomplish the 'journey' and redefine their roles and identity.

Here, one may be tempted to visualise the process of change in women's roles as a passage from private to public. In other words, one tends to say that with modernisation, women are able to step into the public sphere which had hitherto been the male domain, and that, by doing so, they are no longer seen as belonging to the private sphere. This would not be accurate, and for two reasons. Firstly, it is not exact to say that in traditional society women are confined to the private sphere: we have seen that they do have access to some kind of public sphere (through visiting) and that they may achieve some power over decision-making in society. Secondly and more importantly, it is not completely accurate to maintain that in traditional society the public sphere is the male domain; the public does not really exist as a sphere differentiated into supra-familial institutions of 'public interest'. The few public institutions that do exist in a traditional society are accessible to only the upper and middle strata, in the same way as, in a transitional situation, it is the upper and middle strata who can best take advantage of the emerging opportunities to participate in new institutions. Therefore, the access of both men and women to the public is determined, not by the simple criterion of sex, but by the more complex factor of social stratification. In a society where access to political roles and decision-making is not evenly distributed, lower-class men *and* women are deprived of the public, whereas upper-class and middle-class women can have some — even if indirect — access to it. Consequently, the existence of new role opportunities for women would seem to be part of a societal process: the emergence of institutions in the public sphere. In a transitional situation such as Yemen, kinship ceases to be the main principle of social organisation but becomes one among other equally important factors. And there coexist, along with traditional roles based on kinship, other roles based upon the new, supra-familial institutions. Thus it is possible to agree with Evans-Pritchard (1965, p. 55) that what changes with modernisation is not so much 'the relative position of the sexes, as the status — in the broadest sense of the word — of the person as such, whether male or female, and consequently the status of the woman as a person'.

II. The Desertion of Tradition

With the emergence of the public sphere and of the institutions that define it, the traditional world loses some of its relevance. One may say that traditional female groupings are being gradually 'deserted' because of opportunities for involvement in other activities and groups.

In traditional society, unmarried girls are part of an inter-generational world in which their mothers, aunts and grand-mothers partake, and in which differences such as education are not the bases for internal segmentation. With the increase of education, girls become part of peer-groups structured according to age and educational level, and a schoolgirl subculture is now emerging, from which older women are excluded.[7] Whereas in traditional culture the separation between age groups is de-emphasised, in a transitional situation it comes to be stressed, to the point of becoming the basis of a real cleavage. Also, in traditional society every woman possesses all the skills necessary to take care of a house and children, the distribution of knowledge is homo-geneous. Now, discrepancies in knowledge and skills are emerging: not every woman knows, for instance, what stu-dents or nurses or doctors learn, and some may even have a very limited idea of what these roles entail.[8] Knowledge becomes segmented, a hierarchy of experts emerges and people who do not share the same knowledge may begin to inhabit different worlds.

The increase in girls' education tends to stress the social difference between girls and women, and results in a situation wherein girls of different kin groups come to have more in common than girls and women of the same kin groups. At afternoon visits, schoolgirls do not seem to like sitting in the main room (*majlis*) where women are gathered, but prefer a smaller room where they can chat and joke more freely among themselves. The cleavage between the two groups can be expressed once again in Goffman's terms of the opposition between the main 'frontstage' and the 'back-stage'. It can also be expressed at other times by 'code switch-ing', another of Goffman's terms. Thus, the arrival of a married female visitor into a gathering of schoolgirls can cause a considerable change in the atmosphere; once when this occurred, as soon as the woman came into the room and sat down, laughter ceased, conversation became constrained, and, after the preliminary greetings, none of the girls could find anything to talk about with the woman who remained silent while some of the girls whispered to one another. This situation was noticeable since in traditional culture it happens that women receive visits from other women unknown to the group, but without any of the disturbing stiffness and awkwardness that prevails in an 'invaded backstage'.

These two instances showing the separation between age groups cannot be sufficiently explained by invoking traditional patterns of respect of girls towards married women. The point is that schoolgirls are aware that they cannot freely share their common experience in the presence of uneducated married women. Whereas in traditional culture girls and women of all ages may share their experiences, in a modernising situation and with the increase of school attendance, a new phenomenon is emerging in Yemen which is comparable to what has been called in the West the 'generation gap'. The experience of a modern educational system accentuates the uneasiness which may everywhere characterise relations between age groups. This separation becomes even clearer with the intrusion of Western pop music into the traditional *tafriṭa*. I encountered this incongruous pattern only once in 1974 and much more frequently in 1976. When younger girls insist on playing English or French songs (the words of which they themselves do not understand), the whole climate of the visit is changed. Older women begin to exchange looks and hand gestures indicating their inability to understand how anybody could like such unfamiliar tunes and they laugh, perhaps out of embarrassment, at this strange and confusing experience.

Because of outside intrusions and alternatives, the traditional symbolic universe comes to be only one among other possible worlds and women come to experience it in various ways and degrees. Those among my informants who were studying or working could not be at home when housework was to be done. A number of them were in fact housewives, but had another occupation at the same time. Therefore, they had to delegate their domestic responsibilitites either to a female relative if they lived in an extended household or to a maid. Four of my unmarried informants were employed outside the home and nine were students; none of them could help their mothers with housework, except on Fridays. It is obvious that in all such cases the networks of female relatives who share housework are weakened and even cease to exist.

Moreover, housework is no longer seen as an inevitable part of the woman's condition, but only one among other activities, sometimes even an obligation to reduce to a minimum. Working women who live in nuclear familes cannot delegate housework to a female relative, and they attempt to reduce the amount of time they spend on it; they do not often cook traditional and time-consuming dishes, and sometimes altogether eliminate the pattern of the midday meal as the central meal because the evening is the only time they can prepare food. In the daily schedule of modernising Yemeni women, domestic duties must be fitted in with the school, the hospital or the office, and in some cases they no longer take priority over outside activities.

The same is true for the duty of visiting. Those among my informants who were employed outside the home all said that they rarely went to *tafriṭa* and only on very special occasions so as not to hurt people's feelings. Schoolgirls too try to avoid formal visits; they prefer to be among themselves rather than go to *tafriṭa* where older women are present. The reasons generally given for not going to *tafriṭa* include: lack of time, fatigue after a morning's work, not liking the crowdedness and heat of the atmosphere, and being bored with 'just sitting there' for hours. For modernising women, *tafriṭa* is no longer experienced as the most enjoyable and exciting part of the day; it has become a social duty that cannot be completely avoided, a concession made to friends and relatives — and tradition.

Thus, an institution that was fundamental in maintaining the reality of the traditional universe can no longer keep its central place. The women's separate sphere, of which *tafriṭa* was the symbol, no longer constitutes the main context of social experience. And the woman's life, instead of being that integrated whole where work and leisure, domestic and extrafamilial activities alternate without rigid boundaries, is now beginning to be compartmentalised into sectors that are relatively independent of one another.

III. A 'Pluralised' Society[9]

As the San'ani woman's life becomes compartmentalised, those kin-based institutions that were central in traditional culture come to be merely one sector of social life, while modern institutions come to constitute relatively autonomous subworlds. This represents the beginning of the 'pluralisation of social life-worlds', a main characteristic of modernity. Life becomes segmented and the same symbols no longer permeate the various sectors of life (Berger *et al.*, 1974, p. 63). Communication is no longer restricted to the spheres of kinship, neighbourhood and traditional ritual — all inward-directed networks — but is transmitted through a multiplicity of channels. Through the mass media as well as through direct contacts with other cultures, there is a wider confrontation between the native culture and the outside world.

The press, both Yemeni and foreign publications, the various radio programmes, and more importantly television, are important channels linking the outside world with the domestic sphere. 'Knowledge' about society is thus expanded to encompass other times and places and women become more directly aware of 'otherness' and of the social problems of others outside the world of kin. They are encouraged to compare their own problems with those of others and to interpret them as a part of broader social processes. This stimulates reflection upon the relationship between particular events and socio-historical conditions and represents perhaps a rudimentary form of what C. Wright Mills referred to as the 'sociological imagination': the ability to relate particular biographical events to general historical ones (1959, p. 7).

If the mass media make women conscious of actual alternatives for living and rationalising one's life, these alternatives become even more real for those women who have had an opportunity to travel abroad[10] and for those who frequently come into contact with women of the foreign community in San'a. The actual experience of 'otherness' clearly demonstrates that the traditional life and its symbolic universe are less than inevitable, and that other frameworks for living have validity. Individuals or groups may be tempted to 'emigrate' from the traditional universe or even to change the old order altogether (Berger and Luckman, 1971, pp. 125-6).

Thus, there is no longer a fixed symbolic universe for women in which all may participate; nor is there a well-defined female status limiting all other possible statuses, nor a typical life-career to which almost all conform. Rather, there are various possibilities for designing one's life, various 'openings' for shaping one's identity. San'ani girls may begin to think about what they would like to do in the future: how much they want to study, when they wish to get married, whether they will have children or not. One sixteen-year-old girl who was getting married to her cousin said that she had agreed to marry him on the condition that he let her study after they were married; she wanted to become a journalist. A thirteen-year-old schoolgirl said she wanted to get married but not before the age of twenty-four when she finishes her university studies; also, she said, she wanted no children. Some of my married informants had planned to continue their studies after marriage, but had had children immediately and postponed their studies. One sixteen-year-old schoolgirl said she wanted to study architecture, even though there was no school of architecture in the Yemen. The point here is not the extent to which girls actually control their future, but rather that they wish to do so, and that they form future plans in which they project themselves as a different person. Parents as well are making projects for their daughters. The 'openness' and liberalism that characterise some parents' attitudes in this respect was surprising more than once, especially in view of the fact that often there is very little in the parents' own lives that departs from tradition.[11] One illiterate father told me he wished his daughter would get an education and choose her own husband, preferably a foreigner. One mother said she would encourage her daughter to study and become an airplane pilot. Several mothers who were very strict about their own veiling — one of them was the wife of a prominent tribal *shaikh* — said that their daughters would not wear a veil when they were ten. Here again, the point is not whether these statements are an accurate description of what parents would do in reality. Rather such statements indicate an awareness that values valid in one's own case may no longer be so for the next generation. Women of my sample seemed aware that their daughters would be women different from themselves.

Projecting oneself or others into the future as a different person, what Berger refers to as 'life-planning', is a typically modern preoccupation. The individual is aware that he can make decisions that could change his future, and redefine himself as another person. Some of the young women I encountered had changed their career plans several times. One had studied nursing, received her diploma, and worked in a hospital, and then decided to go back to school and study further.[12] Another girl worked as a nurse and then moved to a commercial company while continuing secondary school. A third one, who had been married at eleven and then divorced, studied nursing, worked in a hospital, and then decided to go back to school. However after she was offered a scholarship to pursue her nursing studies in Syria, she changed her mind about secondary school and after much hesitation, she opted for the scholarship and the adventure of living abroad.

Thus, whereas in the traditional world the individual's biography is a given that is already plotted, with modernisation, by contrast, it becomes a design, 'a migration through different social worlds and a successive realisation of a number of possible identities' (Berger *et al.*, 1974, p. 73). To understand such changing itineraries in terms of changing values and identities is the subject of the next chapter.

Notes

1. See Youssef, 1974, for a comparative view of women and work in developing countries.

2. The Chinese-textile factory offers its female employees the services of a nursery (run by British social workers in 1974) where children are attended to while the mothers are at work.

3. Central Planning Organization, *Statistics Book*, San'a 1973 and 1976.

4. They came, by order of importance, from the USSR, China, Italy, Hungary and France.

5. According to the Central Planning Organization *Statistics Book* for 1973, 716 of all foreign teachers come from Arab countries (by order of importance, Egypt, Iraq, Palestine, Syria, Jordan). The rest come from China, the USSR, the UK, India and a category labelled 'others' (which probaly includes a substantial number of American Peace Corps who started coming to Yemen in 1973).

6. This expression is taken from Simmel's description of the stranger (1950, p. 404); it has seemed useful to describe the position of the cultural broker who is both a member and a stranger in his own culture.

7. It is interesting to note that this schoolgirl subculture may breach the norms that are traditionally binding upon unmarried girls. For instance, whereas in traditional culture only married women may chew *qāt*, now an increasing number of schoolgirls chew it occasionally under the pretext that it helps them stay awake when studying for exams.

8. One might even argue that part of the prestige of modern 'experts' is related to the ignorance of the rest of the people about what these experts actually do (see Berger *et al.*, 1974). Parents also may completely ignore what their children do at school. One of my informants was so impressed with her son's gradebook from school, that she did not even realise that he had been required to repeat a year. The prestige of the very act of getting grades was such that the grades themselves became secondary; the mother gave her son a present and was proud to show the gradebook to her friends and relatives.

9. I am using 'pluralised' here in the sense that Berger uses it when he discusses the 'pluralization of social life-worlds' (1974), by which he means the fragmentation of the symbolic universe and the loss of its 'massive reality' as a result of modernisation.

10. Eleven of my informants have been outside Yemen to countries including Algeria, Egypt, England, Lebanon, Somaliland and the USSR.

11. Of course, parents' attitudes may not express what they would actually do when they would be faced with a choice. What is significant is that they express their wishes about, or at least their awareness of, future options outside the traditional options marked by the 'normal' life-cycle.

12. In San'a one may enter the nursing school after primary school; it is thus possible to go back to secondary school after having completed one's nursing studies.

4   CHANGING WOMEN: THE CRITICAL ATTITUDE

'Or, vivre est, en orient,
une idée neuve.'
(Berque, 1969)

I. On Crises

Social change in a transitional society is better understood by
focusing upon the micro-level of experience and investigating
how the phenomenon is 'lived' at the individual level. It is
at definable critical points that the dialectic of traditional
and modern forces is most dramatically revealed. Crises are
those turning points, or social 'passages', in the life of individuals. They may be socially defined and ritually expressed, or
subjectively apprehended as tensions, hesitations or resolu-
tions in the face of decisions that are likely to alter the
subsequent course of one's life. In Yemeni culture,
'social' crises include marriage, childbirth, sickness and death;
'subjectively defined' crises might include decisions to leave
one's occupation, not to marry again, to divorce, or to stop
wearing the veil. Both are important factors in changing the
world view and life plan of those individuals who experience
them. Consequently they may also change the socially available options and legitimations inherent in the system. It
seems that the notion of life crisis is an important concept
for understanding the relationship of subjective and objective
aspects of society and micro-and macro-levels of change.[1]

Every society defines symbolically the passage of the individual from one life status to another. In order to deal with
the potential disorder and breakdown in reality involved in
such situations, the norms governing behaviour at these
passages are clearly spelt out and the transfer is highly ritualised. Rites of passage,[2] following a typical sequence from
separation through reintegration, express and legitimate the
change in status, for the individual and for the community.
In traditional society, every individual life follows a clearly
traced sequence; little variation is possible from the 'normal'
life. In the case of San'ani women, the typical progression

goes from infancy, childhood and puberty, to married life and motherhood. It is marked by well-defined passage rites: starting to wear the veil, wedding and childbirth rituals, and, in some cases, divorce and remarriage. Since there are no alternatives to this life sequence,[3] it becomes, 'massively real' to all members of the society. Even transitions which, in principle, involve the risk of a breakdown come to be routinised and even taken for granted.

Crisis and adaptation to crisis are seen clearly in the case of the initial marriage in San'a. Some women say how sad they were when they heard that their parents had decided to betroth them. A number of them add: 'But I was *jāhila* [ignorant].[4] Later when I saw that my husband was good to me, I became used to marriage and now I am *murtāḥa* [contented, satisfied].' In other words, the individual looking back at her life, is reassured in that she has followed the socially desirable sequence. Those turning points which at the time seemed — and objectively were — painful breaks are reinterpreted in the light of later developments as necessary stages in a progression. They are not only necessary in the philosophical sense, but also good. Thus one woman who had described her sorrow at the news of her marriage, seven years before, tried to convince one of her friends that she should not refuse to get married because marriage, she said, was the most beautiful thing in life (*zīnat al ḥayāt*). In 'normal times', then, the crisis can be dealt with successfully: the individual accepts the objective realities and internalises the socially given legitimations attached to the institutional order; 'he can reassure himself that he is living correctly' (Berger and Luckman, 1971, p. 117).

II. Critical Experiences: Disruption and Redirection

In some cases however, cultural legitimations are not sufficiently powerful to ensure a smooth passage from one stage to the other, and the critical break may be too great for a real 'passage' to be achieved. The crisis cannot be resolved by routine means and thus comes to constitute a point of fundamental cleavage, a real turning point.

The main socially defined crisis points in the life of a San'ani woman are marriage and childbirth: they mark the two status changes which generally take place in the life of every female: from girl to married woman and from wife to mother. These two crisis points can be, and often are, the source of much conflict and suffering. Even though traditional culture provides women with opportunities to manipulate situations to their advantage, this is not to say that women can always do so. Often girls are victims of social arrangements which violate human integrity and leave no room for individual choice.

It is not uncommon in Yemen for girls to be married at the age of eight, nine or ten. The husband may be as young as nine or ten, and as old as fifty. The physical costs of marriage under such conditions may be considerable. According to one non-Yemeni midwife with a long experience in an obstetrics and gynaecology ward, a number of young girls suffer painful and often irreparable damage because their bodies are not sufficiently formed when they first enter into sexual relations. A number of young women, already physically weak,[5] are endangered by early and repeated pregnancies. Often an early pregnancy and miscarriage can definitely damage reproductive functions: then, to the shock of an early marriage is added that of being repudiated because, in many cases, the husband cannot accept the fact that his wife is unable to bear children. The male's social status takes precedence over the female's physical state. Moreover, marriage conditions are such that the risks of incompatibility between spouses are high, and sometimes lead to tragic consequences. One woman was married very early and against her will. The man, she found out, was not only very old, but also mentally ill. Many girls escape their new husband's house after a few days or weeks of married life and attempt to return home. Some of them experience severe shock after marriage and are disturbed for the rest of their lives.

In traditional San'ani society, such crises would be interpreted as resulting from the 'nature' of certain individuals rather than from particular social arrangements. For instance, the negative consequences of early marriage are not seen as the injustice of society, but are imputed to the fact that some individuals exploit certain social situations for their own private interest. One woman said to me: 'Early marriage is bad when some parents are so greedy for the *mahr* [bride-price] that they force their daughter to get married even before she is nubile.' Bad marriages and divorce are attributed to the incompatible natures of partners rather than to the social conditions of marriage which do not permit previous familiarity, and thus increase the risks of incompatibility.

Traditional thinking in San'a sees conflicts in a particularistic fashion, as the product of personal characteristics and, therefore, to be dealt with through personal negotiation rather than a general reordering of relationships. During a discussion on marriage patterns, divorce and polygyny, I asked one woman how, given such conditions, marriages generally worked. She replied: 'The Yemeni woman has a great capacity for endurance and patience [*quwwat ṣabr*].' Implied is the idea that individuals adapt to the conditions of life, that they do not question them. When there are no available alternatives, the general validity of cultural norms remains unchallenged: the social system is a 'given', and the problems that emerge are seen as inevitable components of all lives rather than as the product of contingent social arrangements, and least of all as a matter of unfairness or exploitation.

In a modernising society by contrast, the confrontation with other worlds challenges the inevitability of the traditional world: 'Pluralism encourages both skepticism and innovation and is thus inherently subversive of the taken-for-granted reality of the traditional status quo' (Berger and Luckman, 1971, p. 143). Some San'ani women begin to look back at their own lives and evaluate them critically. One widow in her late thirties who had been married at thirteen against her will said that she actually never liked the life she lived with her husband even though he had been good to her: she only stayed with him because it was a habit (*'āda*). Another woman who had already been married nine years said she still was afraid of conjugal life, and was not satisfied with it. Life conditions are becoming the subject of critical reflection: they are not necessary or inescapable. In transitional situations, crises can no longer remain routinised but rather come to constitute dynamic points at which the potential for disruption and change is the greatest. Objective conditions are re-examined, and the individual becomes aware that he has the choice to redirect his life. There come to exist chances for decision-making which not only transcend traditional patterns, but also undermine them.

Cases of redirection closely following a crisis in the biographical sequence indicate that this is a period of crucial decision-making. Almost half of the women I interviewed who had an occupation outside the home had started to work after a period of crisis in their lives. One of them had had an unhappy marriage — a marriage which she herself had wanted — until the time of the 1962 Revolution. Then, constant political upheavals apparently affected the mental health of her husband who began to show occasional symptoms of paranoia. She, however, chose not to leave him, even though her family was pressing her to do so. After she had taken a definite decision to stay with him in spite of all, she also started working as a nurse: her new occupation provided her with a kind of escape from a situation that was making her suffer.[6] It also provided a substantial contribution to the family income. Another woman who had been married against her will to an elderly man also mentally disturbed obtained a divorce after less than a year, entered the nursing school and then took up hospital duties. Yet another girl had been married at age eleven. Her in-laws made trouble for her, and her husband 'unjustly' wrote the first of the three repudiation papers; and so she obtained a divorce, studied nursing and started working. In these cases, successive crises result in a complete redirection of the person's life. The redirection, however, can also be the result, not of repeated crises, but of a 'non-crisis', that is, the lack of passage through a socially desirable stage. One of my informants was a woman in her mid-thirties and still unmarried. She had begun to study nursing and to work in a hospital after she realised she was past marriage age and had to seek another course for her life.

The relationship between socially defined crises and subsequent redirection varies and can be quite dramatic, as was the case of one girl who had obtained a divorce shortly after marriage, while pregnant. Refusing all her husband's pressing requests for her to return, she studied nursing until the time of her delivery. When nursing diplomas were being officially distributed to students, a friend of hers, completely veiled in the black *sharshaf* like all other girls present, accepted the diploma in her name; on that very day, her daughter was born. The two passages, the one to motherhood and the one marking the beginning of her 'nurse status', occurred simultaneously. Acute socially defined turning points represent also a potential identity crisis in which the individual may choose to redefine herself in the process. In the case above, this girl later refused the role of mother: she left her newborn daughter to her own mother's care, only seeing her after work to the extent that the little girl called the grandmother '*māma*' (mother). The mother preferred the relatively freer position of a young divorced woman with an occupation. She thus chose a new identity for herself, and 'migrated' to another world:

In light of these cases, we can appreciate the statement made by a woman in her thirties, married very early against her will. Asked about the major social change since the Revolution, she replied: 'Before there was *ghaṣb* [forcing people], now people have some choice.' One way to express the change from tradition to modernity is in terms of increased alternatives for action and potential for self-fulfilment.

Another crucial point also becomes apparent here: that the appeal of new alternatives is strongest for those who have suffered most from traditional conflicts and restrictions, who have been most threatened and harmed in their bodies, self-apprehensions and self-esteem. One of Bastide's comments about acculturation is also descriptive of modernisation in Yemen: 'It is precisely because they are maladjusted and have personal conflicts they cannot resolve in terms of their own customs that these people will tend to imitate foreigners to see if their customs will allow them to find a resolution to their own dissatisfactions' (1973, p. 99).

III. Commuters and Outsiders

Maladjustment and unhappy experiences are not, of course, the only factors in the rise of an attitude critical of tradition. Some people, because of their socialisation process, come to 'inhabit' a world that is not typically the traditional universe and hence they may become aware of the contingency of social arrangements. The mediation of discrepant worlds in

the course of socialisation is a characteristic of complex
societies with a differentiated distribution of knowledge. In
traditional San'ani society, any discrepant socialisation
would be mainly the result of having lived outside the country
for a period, or of having grown up in a family which, for
various reasons, did not live in total conformity with traditional ways.

Among my informants,[7] six had lived abroad for some
time because their fathers or husbands were government
officials in Egypt, England, Somaliland or the USSR. Five
had travelled outside Yemen for a month or more on holiday
trips (to Egypt, Lebanon or Algeria) accompanied by a member of their family or a person to whom the family delegated
the responsibility to sponsor their daughter. Four had experienced what seems to have been a relatively liberal socialisation process; the grandfather of two of these had been
involved in the 1962 Revolution and had participated in the
overthrow of the Imamate, these two sisters were never
forced to wear the veil. Two other girls were the daughters of
a Yemeni journalist who had travelled extensively and seems
to have been in favour of changing the condition of Yemeni
women. He had encouraged his daughters not to wear the
veil, and they did not, until his premature death, when
'social pressures', as they said, forced them to wear it again.

Individuals who experience discrepant universes in the
course of their lives are likely to become conscious of the
relativity of norms. For instance, none of my informants who
had been abroad had worn the veil outside Yemen, but all
did when they came back; all explained to me that, whereas
the veil still offered some protection in Yemen, it was not
suitable in other countries. Implied here is the idea that the
same symbol does not have the same meaning in different
contexts and that there are situations where the most widely
accepted norms do not apply. When society becomes 'pluralised' into subworlds some individuals begin to shift and to
change completely their 'presentation of self' according to
the context. For instance, two wives of high-ranking political
figures, told me that they wore different styles of dresses,
some typical San'ani, others Western, depending on whether
they attend a traditional *tafriṭa* or are visiting where foreigners

are present. It is interesting that individuals who do shift between different subworlds may wish to signal, for one reason or another, the fact that they 'shift'. Yet another wife of a high government official who had lived in Europe and the USSR combined traditional Yemeni with Western style dress. At the *tafriṭa* where I met her she was the only San'ani woman who wore conspicuously Parisian-style shoes to signal her standing outside the traditional world while still participating in it. Similarly, girls who live in Aden (South Yemen) for part of the year go to the *tafriṭa* wearing the transparent Adeni dress rather than the heavy brocade San'ani dress. Through their behaviour, they evidently wish to convey the idea that, though they do go to *tafriṭa* like other San'ani women, they also participate in other worlds. 'Commuters', if we may use the term to refer to those individuals who alternate between subworlds, consciously or unconsciously demonstrate the status attached to having access to other alternatives. They may be 'like the rest', but they are also different. 'Commuters' make people aware that their own way of life is not the only one, that it may not even be the best. They stimulate a process of emulation and achieve in part what cultural brokers do, that is, provide a nexus between traditional and modern status spheres and set the stage for a new awareness of society itself.

Thus, in Yemen today, several forces converge to project a new level of consciousness. The critical attitude is shaped by the interplay of three factors: the existence of crises which individuals experience, the availability of alternative ways of living, and the presence of individuals or institutions which help reinterpret traditional conflicts in the light of modern opportunities. We discussed these as traditional 'passages', crisis situations, redirection of life and career, 'commuters' and the confrontation with discordant realities. The critical attitude is characteristic of transitional and modern societies, even though adumbrations of it may exist in traditional or primitive societies (Radin, 1957). It is defined in opposition to the attitude of 'unreflected "being at home" in the social world' (Berger, 1974, p. 74). Critical individuals can translate their own and the peculiar problems of others into a general 'theory' (in the sociology of knowledge sense) of society, rather than accepting them as the inevitable results of 'human nature.[8] Traditional crises provide the starting point for reflection and encourage critical individuals to challenge traditional conditions and orient themselves towards modern alternatives, and thus attempt to redefine norms and values with reference to another model of the 'good' or the 'better' life.

IV. Redefining Women

The conceptual and moral bases of this process of critical rethinking are to be found in the prevalent images of women as they are communicated through the mass media and literature, because these images both express and shape the social perception of women. They also constitute 'ideal types', in the Weberian sense, and models with reference to which the performance of women and their patterns of behaviour are evaluated. An examination of statements about women by women and men cluster around certain cultural types: the mother, the wife, the lover, the woman with an occupation, the woman as Muslim, the woman as citizen.

In the radio, newspapers and, recently, television of San'a, the mother as an ideal type is repeatedly described as the basis of society and her importance is rationalised by the Koranic injunction to honour both parents and by the universal need of all creatures for maternal love and care. On the occasion of the newly celebrated Mother's Day, an article in *Al Thawra*, the leading daily, reaffirmed the role of the mother as one that is not inferior to the roles of men, since men can never replace women as mothers. The article stressed the significance of the educational function of mothers and how it contributes to social stability. The Family Radio Programme also emphasises the importance of being a good mother, and the consequences upon children's personalities of poor care on the part of mothers, often giving advice on how to take care of children. In general, there is an increasing concern about the role of the mother in society, a positive evaluation and idealisation — perhaps even a defence —of this role. This is a new phenomenon.

In traditional Yemeni culture, as in all tribal-based societies, the mother is the central femine role. But the mother emerges as a conscious ideal precisely when society begins to move away from a purely tribal social structure, when, rather than being silently taken for granted, the role of mother becomes a topic of reflection and discussion. In Berque's esoteric words, 'the theme [of the mother] is born when the person discovers his existence not only through the proud assertion of a genealogy, but through the living continuity of woman' (1969, p. 202). To simplify — while perhaps distorting — Berque's thought, the mother-as-ideal comes into being when the person is not only seen as an element in a kinship system, but arises as an autonomous reality. Paradoxically here, when motherhood is expressed as a cultural ideal, this represents the beginning of the liberation of the female from the role of mother as the only choice. The appearance of the mother as ideal type indicates that the social conditions, in which the role of mother is the only alternative for all women, are changing. It is the starting point of reflection about more dynamic feminine ideals.

The conditions of marriage in traditional Yemeni culture do not emphasise the wife as a feminine type. With modernisation, there is a shift in emphasis from the role of mother to that of wife and from parent-child to husband-wife bonds, which has been referred to as the 'conjugalization' process (Peacock and Kirsch, 1973). In San'a the mass media are giving increased attention to the conjugal bond. For instance, the Family Radio Programme often gives women advice on how to be good wives and how to have a good relationship with their husbands. Aspects of the conjugal relation which would, in a traditional society, only be mentioned among women are dealt with in the press and radio. Conjugal life is described as sacred and requiring the couple's full concern. One article in *Al Thawra* even maintained that spouses should spend their leisure time together rather than separately; the author, a female, wrote that the wife needs as much, if not more, relaxation as her husband, and that he should stay at home with her and not go out alone.

Another theme related to the conjugalisation process is the growing independence of the new couple from in-laws, and this affects the whole network of traditional kinship relations. *Al Thawra* devoted a whole article to this issue. The Family Radio Programme in one of its sessions dramatised the problem of the mother who attempts to keep her son under control and threatens his conjugal relationship. In the play, the two spouses, in the end, realised that the mother's interference was undermining their otherwise good relationship and they decided to keep her out of their conjugal life, without, however, rejecting her altogether. The trend away from the extended family is not new in Yemeni culture. Most of my informants, asked about the causes of divorce, answered that in-laws were almost always responsible for marital problems. One woman told me: 'The best thing is to marry a *yatīm* [orphan], for he has no in-laws to bother you, and especially no avaricious and nosy mother-in-law.' Criticisms of in-laws are not a result of modernisation only. What is new, however, is the approach to the husband-wife relation: the necessity for their being independent is expressed not in terms of the trouble caused by in-laws as a group, but rather in terms of the rights of two individuals to have some independence and privacy, and a personal relationship.[9]

From the wife as feminine ideal to the lover the transition can be easily effected. Perhaps it is more accurate to say that as feminine ideals they can seldom be separated, for both are based on the notion of a personal dyadic relationship with a strongly emotional content and one which is, in theory at least, exclusive. But the theme of the lover, because it is seen as deviating from social norms tends to be expressed in music and poetry rather than other media. In fact, the traditional San'ani art of singing and playing the *'ūd* (lute) can become a vehicle for new emotions and values.[10] One girl who had learned to play the *'ūd* composed her own songs which she sang for me. They were about friends, about an imaginary and distant lover, about loneliness and melancholy — themes that are part of romantic songs everywhere. The development of popular music has important implications for cultural images and values. It 'carries to the heart of forbidden homes widely spread emotions and it provides the woman with sentimental models which nourish her and which she in turn nourishes with her personal feelings' (Berque, 1969, p. 210).

Perhaps more powerful is the impact of television. By bombarding San'ani homes with a variety of discrepant feminine roles (the Cairene bourgeois lady, the veiled Gulf girl, the American housewife, the student, the maid, the peasant woman, the matron, the fiancée, as well as the belly-dancer, the actress and the modern singer) and of contradictory images of women (the faithful wife, the vain young girl, the depraved woman, the obedient daughter, the career woman, the pious Muslim, the cunning seductress), television contributes to undermining traditional cultural ideas and offering a multiplicity of alternative models.

As a result, there are various attempts to make sense of the changing realities of woman's roles and images by having recourse to religious or national ideologies. Allowing women to get an education and to take an occupation outside the home is justified as a contribution to national development. Women are citizens, said an article in *Al Thawra*, and should help build their country. Since the constitution of Yemen grants men and women the right to work, it is seen as a national duty to place one's skill at the service of social development.

At other times, women's new roles in society are rational-ised with reference to religious values. Many debates about women are built around the concept of woman as a Muslim and her consequent rights and duties. One newspaper article reaffirmed the idea that Islam addresses itself to all human beings, be they men or women, and that women are endowed with both rationality and moral judgement. Examples were presented from the Prophet's days of women who contribu-ted to the development and spread of Islam through their role in *jihād* (holy war), through their opinions about religious issues and through advising men. The three most commonly presented examples are those of Khadīja and 'Aisha, the Prophet's wives, and Zaynab, the daughter of Ali. These women who are revered by all Muslims are used as culture heroes to legitimate the changing activities of women in a changing society.

Implied in most of the legitimations defining new femin-ine types is the idea that, by performing their duties and exer-cising their rights in relation to new roles, women contribute both to their personal happiness and to social welfare. However, when the emphasis is put on the individual rather than on the society, this may constitute a break away from the optimistic, even conservative philosophy which assumes a close relationship between personal and social development. Under the title 'Woman and her Social Rights', one article in the newspaper *San'a* justified changes in the social condition of the female by affirming that 'woman was not created for sex and is no longer a *ḥurma*[11] but a human being! The woman is a person, that is, someone with a mind and emotions just like men.' Another article in *Al Thawra* maintained that a woman's life should be directed towards experience and personal fulfilment. This is in clear contrast with the traditional value of *rāḥa* (rest, comfort, contentment) which was, for many San'ani women the most desirable condition and the standard with reference to which many of their judgements were made. In other words, traditionally, situations are evaluated according to whether they bring *rāḥa* to the individual, or else create *ta'ab* (trouble, hardship, fatigue). This static, perhaps negative, approach is gradually being challenged by ideas of love, experience, self-fulfilment, liberation, all values based on an individualistic ethic defined in opposition to social constraints.

It is in poetry that these changes and dilemmas are most vividly expressed.[12] Mainly in the work of the Yemeni poet Muhammad al Sharafī we encounter poems about women; some address them directly, others are presented as the discourse of women using the first person.[13] His work is popular with the young, even though his audacity provokes the horror of traditional *'ulama* (men of religion). He writes about all the diverse and often discordant female types, about pure adolescent girls, resigned mothers, simple village women and debauched women. 'Woman Without Love', 'A Vulgar Woman', 'When Sex becomes a Trade', and 'The Naked City' are some titles of his poems. Love is sex and depravity, but it is also an ideal and even a religion:

> My idol
> If I had a religion and a god
> You are my religion and my god

> If I have a fault
> You forgive
> For you are my pardon and my fault
> And if I suffer pain
> You heal
> For you are my suffering and my cure

One of his main sources of inspiration is the veil because it can be used to symbolically express the contradictions that exist in Yemeni culture, about women and about the person in general. The veil is an obstacle to interaction, a barrier between lovers and a symbol of all the constraints that society imposes on the women:

> Do I see a woman
> Or a heap of sadness
> Telling the perfidy of years
>
> How they bury her miserable existence
> And theirs is the one to be buried

and of the hypocrisy of social customs:

> O Mother if my virtue is my veil
> Must I honour it and men are not honourable?

But it is also a symbol of woman's mystery and charm and of the desire she arouses:

> Your black veil entices me
> Opens me to the hunger of desire and envelops me
> It hides the sun behind it
> And conceals the radiant moon and the breaking
>   dawn behind it
> And almost divulges its light behind the night.

Behind the veil is the passive acceptance of repression, but also powerful passions:

> Let him see me without a veil
> Smell my perfume and reap my fruits
> I am a woman, in my blood is
> A violent spring which fears autumn nights

The veil is the instrument of oppression, but at the same time it is the incitement to liberation:

> For I have rejected their ignorance
> Laughed at them for what they do
> And I came out unveiled

It is a key symbol and as such is essentially linked to a deep cultural dialectic. Only poetry, it seems, could anticipate and express the dynamic of this potential transformation:

> What is a woman's worth,
> Who did not break a chain
> Destroy a prison
> Tear all veils.

Notes

1. Berger and Luckman (1971), draw attention to the importance of crises occurring in the course of the individual's socialisation process, for the maintenance and transformation of the institutional order.

2. This term of Van Gennep (1960), Douglas (1966) and Turner (1967) have expanded and innovated upon in their analysis of the structure and meaning of the 'rite de passage'.

3. The existing alternative, namely, not to get married, is considered an 'anomaly' (see Chapter 1), and consequently is not really an alternative.

4. It is interesting to note that the plural *juhhāl* is used in Yemen to designate children generally.

5. According to a Yemeni female doctor, due to lack of awareness, the wife's deficient physical condition only comes to her and her husband's notice in cases of sterility.

6. This necessity to escape her situation was also apparent in the fact that she was one of the few women I met who said she could not do without chewing *qāt* daily. She needed *qāt*, she added, because she had to have some rest (*rāha*) and forget her problems.

7. A significant number of women (15 out of 40) had had the opportunity to travel or live abroad, or had grown up in atypical families. This again is related to the sample of women interviewed and the fact that it is representative of the middle and upper strata rather than the society as a whole.

8. It should be made clear here that the 'uncritical attitude' is not that of individuals who are unaware of the existence of problems, but who, when confronting problems, impute them to the 'natures' of individuals rather than to the structure of the system.

9. Actually, the conjugal ethic may lead — at least temporarily — to a retraditionalisation of marriage patterns. One of my informants maintained that the increasing frequency of parallel-cousin marriages was related to the fact that boys and girls now wish to know each other before marriage and that cousins are for the time the only ones who have a chance to do so. This statement is worth noting even though the assumption that parallel-cousin marriage is increasing remains unverified.

10. Similarly, as a traditional role, the female singer can become a significant carrier of new attitudes and emotions. One of the two most popular female singers in Yemen who 'commuted' between Aden and San'a with her husband, also a singer, could conceivably influence new female models, both through her life career and through her songs.

11. *Hurma* is the term used for the female in traditional Muslim society. It implies the idea of something forbidden and to be protected.

12. Poetry occupies a central place in Yemeni culture. It is prevalent throughout the society, not only among educated urbanites but also among non-literate tribesmen. Today in San'a, poetry books are continuously published and sold, not just in bookstores but even on the sidewalks of the city by vendors and sometimes by the poets themselves.

13. He may in some respects be compared to the Syrian poet Nizar Kabbani.

CONCLUSION

Even if San'a sleeps on her sorrows awhile
And her stupor and drowsiness are prolonged,
One day her morning will rise against darkness
And a rain will wash away her lethargy.
(A. al-Maqāliḥ)

Modernisation has been analysed here in terms of both the women's perception of society and society's images of women. Traditional society was discussed mainly with reference to the central theme of male dominance and female seclusion. Through an analysis of the everyday life and visiting rituals of San'ani women, I attempted to understand the relationship between cultural ideology and social reality. Where society strictly enforces sex-segregation, the female domain comes to constitute a separate sphere over which males have little authority and from which they are excluded. A deeper examination of the rituals of this female sphere reveals an autonomous female view of the world which not only contradicts the male model but often ridicules its main ideas.

Several forces converge to change the traditional universe of the female. We discussed crises in the individual's life, 'passage points', the confrontation with discordant realities and alternative life-ways, 'brokers' and 'commuters', as factors which contribute to undermine traditional groupings, encourage women gradually to 'desert' them and project a variety of situations in which women define themselves. Thus emerges a new critical attitude which reinterprets traditional conflicts in light of modern opportunities and redefines social options and legitimations.

One recurring theme in our analysis has been the veil, both as a central performance in the traditional world and a key symbol around which the drama of change unfolds. More than anything else, the veil represents the contradictions inherent in Yemeni culture between purity and pollution, strength and weakness, communication and alienation.

Throughout, I have attempted to keep track of both the

societal and the individual dimension of modernisation. I have drawn attention to the ways in which individual women can manipulate situations to their own advantage. In doing so, I am not contesting the coerciveness of the normative order, nor ignoring the real facts of repression in the life of San'ani women. Rather, I have sought to consider things from another perspective and emphasise the role of the person in accepting or changing social reality. In his critique of functionalism, Murphy finds that many theorists work with 'the implicit assumption that they can discard and ignore the fact that the people they study are thinking, plotting, scheming for the future . . . It is far tidier and intellectually easier to see man as helpless in the grips of history and institutions' (1972, p. 109). This is especially true of women, who are seen in most studies as exploited and passive pawns moved about in an oppressive social system. My experience with the culture of North Yemen has allowed me to see another dimension of reality and to consider women as active participants in a culture which, like all cultures, contains ambivalences, contradictions and dissonances.

BIBLIOGRAPHY

Abu Zahra, N. (1970) 'On the Modesty of Women in Arab Muslim Villages: A Reply', *American Anthropologist*, 72:5, October 1970, pp. 1079-92.

Altorki, S. (1973) 'Religion and Social Organization of Elite Families in Urban Saudi Arabia', unpublished Ph.D. dissertation, University of California, Berkeley.

Antoun, R. (1968) 'On the Modesty of Women in Arab Muslim Villages: A Study in the Accomodation of Traditions', *American Anthropologist*, 70:4, August 1968, pp. 671-96.

—— (1972) *Arab Village*, Indiana University Press, Bloomington, London.

Ardener, E. (1972) 'Belief and the Problem of Women', in *The Interpretation of Ritual*, ed. I.S. La Fontaine, Tavistock Publications, London.

Arnaud, T. (1850) 'Les Akhdam de l'Yémen, leur Origine Probable, leurs Moeurs', *Journal Asiatique*, Avril 1850, pp. 376-97.

Baer, G. (1964) *Population and Society in the Arab East*, Praeger, New York, Washington.

Bastide, R. (1973) *Applied Anthropology*, Croom Helm, London.

Berger, P. (1971) *The Social Construction of Reality*, Penguin, Harmondsworth.

Berger, P. *et al.* (1974) *The Homeless Mind*, Penguin, Harmondsworth.

Berque, J. (1969) *Les Arabes d'Hier à Demain*, Seuil, Paris.

Bornstein, A. (1974) *Food and Society in the Yemen Arab Republic*, a Food and Agriculture Organization report, Rome.

Central Planning Organisation (1973) *Statistical Yearbook*, San'a.

—— (1976) *Statistical Yearbook*, San'a.

Chelhod, J. (1973a) 'Parenté et Mariage au Yémen', *L'Ethnographie*, No. 67, pp. 47-90.

—— (1973b), 'Les Cérémonies de Mariage au Yémen', *Objets et Mondes*, xii, pp. 3-34.

Chodorow, N. (1974) 'Family Structure and Feminine Personality', in *Woman, Culture and Society*, ed. M. Rosaldo and L. Lamphere, Stanford University Press, Stanford.

Douglas, M. (1966) *Purity and Danger*, Penguin, Harmondsworth.

Evans-Prichard, E. (1965) *The Position of Women in Primitive Society*, Faber, London.

Fayein, C. (1957) *French Doctor in the Yemen*, Robert Hale Ltd, London.

Fernea, E. (1969) *Guests of the Shaikh*, Anchor Books, New York.

—— (1976) *A Street in Marrakech*, Anchor Books, New York.

Friedl, E. (1967) 'The Position of Women, Appearance and Reality', *Anthropological Quarterly*, 40:3, pp. 89-114.

Fuller, A. (1961) *Buarij: Portrait of a Lebanese Muslim Village*, Harvard University Press, Cambridge, Mass.

Gellner, E. (1964) *Thought and Change*, University of Chicago Press, Chicago.

Gluckman, M. (1955) *Custom and Conflict in Africa*, Free Press, Glencoe, Ill.

Goffman, E. (1971) *The Presentation of Self in Everyday Life*, Penguin, Harmondsworth.

Goode, W. (1970) *World Revolution and Family Patterns*, Free Press, New York.

Hilal, J. (1971) 'The Management of Male Dominance in Traditional Arab Culture', *Civilizations*, 29, pp. 84-95.

Keenan, E. (1974) 'Ins and Outs of Women's Specch', *Cambridge Anthropology*, 1:3, April 1974.

Lane, E. (1863-93) *Arabic-English Lexicon* (8 parts), London.

Leach, E. (1964) *Political Systems of Highland Burma*, Beacon Press, London.

Lutfiyya, A. (1966) *Baytin, a Jordanian Village*, Mouton, The Hague.

Maher, V. (1974) *Women and Property in Morocco*, Cambridge University Press.

Mills, C. Wright (1959) *The Sociological Imagination*, Penguin, Harmondsworth.

Murphy, R. (1961) 'Social Distance and the Veil', *American Anthropologist*, vol. 66, pp. 1257-74.

—— (1972) *The Dialectics of Social Life*, Basic Books, London, New York.

Nelson, C. (1973) 'Women and Power in Nomadic Societies of the Middle East', in *The Desert and the Sown*, ed. C. Nelson, University of California, Berkeley.

Obermeyer, G. (1973a) 'Leadership and Transition in Bedouin Society: a Case Study' in *The Desert and the Sown*, ed. C. Nelson, University of California, Berkeley.

—— (1973b) 'Anthropological Aspects of *qāt* and *qāt* Use in Yemen', a World Health Organization report.

Ortner, S. (1974) 'Is Female to Male as Nature is to Culture?', in *Woman, Culture and Society*, ed. M. Rosaldo and L. Lamphere, Stanford University Press.

Papanek, H. (1973) 'Purdah: Separate Worlds and Symbolic Shelter', *Comparative Studies in Society and History*, 15:3, pp. 289-325.

Patai, R. (1973) *Golden River to Golden Road*, University of Pennsylvania Press.

Peacock, J. and T. Kirsch (1973) *The Human Direction*, Appleton Century Croft, New York.

Peters, E. (1966) 'Consequences of the Segregation of the Sexes among Arabs', unpublished paper delivered at the Mediterranean Social Science Council Conference, Athens.

Radin, P. (1957) *Primitive Man as a Philosopher*, Dover Publications, New York.

Richards, A. (1974) 'The Position of Women: An Anthropological View', *Cambridge Anthropology*, 1:3.

Rosaldo, M. (1974) 'Woman, Culture and Society: a Theoretical Overview', in *Woman, Culture and Society*, ed. M. Rosaldo and L. Lamphere, Stanford University Press.

Saint-Hilaire, A. (1975) *Je reviens du Yémen*, Pensée Moderne, Paris.

Simmel, G. (1950) *The Sociology of Georg Simmel*, ed. K. Wolf, Free Press, New York.

—— (1955) *Conflict and the Web of Group Affiliations*, Free Press, New York.

Tillion, G. (1966) *Le Harem et les Cousins*, Seuil, Paris.

Turner, V. (1967) *The Forest of Symbols*, Cornell University Press.

United Nations (1958 and later) *Statistical Yearbooks*.

—— (1973) 'The Development of Education in Yemen', a United Nations Development Project report.

Van Gennep, A. (1960) *The Rites of Passage*, Routledge and Kegan Paul, London.

Youssef, N. (1974) *Women and Work in Developing Countries*, University of California, Berkeley.

Sources in Arabic

Anonymous, (nd) *Ikhtiyārāt al Imām Ahmed*, unpublished manuscript, San'a.

al Maqālih, A. (1971) *Lā Budda Min San'a* ('There is no Escape from San'a), selected poems, Taiz.

al Murtada, Imam Ahmed B. Yahya (nd) *Kitāb al Azhār*.

al Sharafī, M. (1970) *Dumū' Sharāshif* ('Tears of the Veils'), selected poems, San'a.

—— (1974) *Ma'aha Abadan* ('With Her For Ever'), selected poems, Beirut.

Newspapers and Magazines Published in San'a

Al Thawra
Ma'reb
San'a

INDEX